NAOMI KLEIN

AUTHOR OF *NO LOGO*

FENCES AND WINDOWS

DISPATCHES FROM THE FRONT LINES OF THE GLOBALIZATION DEBATE

PICADOR USA

Fences and Windows

No Logo articulated the concerns of a generation and chronicled a new movement. In doing so it became an international bestseller and was translated into twenty-three languages.

Since its publication Naomi Klein has tirelessly contributed to the contemporary debate on globalization, its impact and its future. *Fences and Windows* brings together two years of commentary written at demonstrations and summits around the world—eyewitness reports from the front lines of the globalization debate. It brings us up-to-date on the protests and possibilities, the hopes for change and the barriers raised against it.

Fences and Windows collects Naomi Klein's most notable articles and speeches, many of them never before published, on such issues as NAFTA, genetically modified organisms and economic fundamentalism. This book also reflects on the nature of resistance: the street protests that have shocked and energized millions, the purpose of carnival-style subversion, and the apparent disorganization that is the movement's great strength.

Provocative, intelligent and passionate, *Fences and Windows* is a survival guide for life in the world economy, a record of globalization and its consequences, and a document, in its own right, of a unique time in our history.

FENCES A

D WINDOWS DISPATCHES FROM

NAOMI KLEIN

THE FRONT LINES OF THE GLOBALIZATION DEBATE

Editor: Debra Ann Levy

PICADOR USA

NEW YORK

A portion of the sales from each copy of this book goes to the Fences and Windows Fund, which provides funds for activist legal defense and popular education.
www.fencesfund.org

www.picadorusa.com

Picador ® is a U.S. registered trademark and is used by St. Martin's Press under license from Pan Books Limited.

For information on Picador USA Reading Group Guides, as well as ordering, please contact the Trade Marketing department at St. Martin's Press.
Phone: 1-800-221-7945 extension 763
Fax: 212-677-7456
E-mail: trademarketing@stmartins.com

ISBN 0-312-30799-3

First published in Canada by Random House of Canada Limited

First Picador USA Edition: October 2002

10 9 8 7 6 5 4 3 2 1

CONTENTS

CONTENTS

IV / Capitalizing on Terror

V / Windows to Democracy

PREFACE

PREFACE

Preface
Fences of Enclosure, Windows of Possibility

This is not a follow up to *No Logo*, the book about the rise of anti-corporate activism that I wrote between 1995 and 1999. That was a thesis-driven research project; *Fences and Windows* is a record of dispatches from the front lines of a battle that exploded right around the time that *No Logo* was published. The book was at the printer's when the largely subterranean movements it chronicled entered into mainstream consciousness in the industrialized world, mostly as a result of the November 1999 World Trade Organization protests in Seattle. Overnight, I found myself tossed into the middle of an international debate over the most pressing question of our time: what values will govern the global age?

What began as a two-week book tour turned into an adventure that spanned two and a half years and twenty-two countries. It took me to tear-gas-filled streets in Quebec City and Prague, to neighbourhood assemblies in Buenos Aires, on camping trips with anti-nuclear activists in the South Australian desert and into formal debates with European heads of state. The four years of investigative seclusion that it took to write *No Logo* had done little to prepare me for this. Despite media reports naming me as one of the "leaders" or "spokespeople" for the global protests, the truth was that I had never been involved in politics and didn't much like crowds. The first time I had to give a speech about globalization, I looked down at my notes, started reading and didn't look up again for an hour and a half.

But this was no time to be shy. Tens and then hundreds of thousands of people were joining new demonstrations each month, many of them people like me who had never really believed in the possibility of political change until now. It seemed as if the failures of the reigning economic model had suddenly become impossible to ignore—and that was before Enron. In the name of meeting the demands of multinational investors, governments the world over were failing to meet the needs of the people who elected them. Some of these unmet needs were basic and urgent—for medicines, housing, land, water; some were less tangible—for non-commercial cultural spaces to communicate, gather and share, whether on the Internet, the public airwaves or the streets. Underpinning it all was the betrayal of the fundamental need for democracies that are responsive and participatory, not bought and paid for by Enron or the International Monetary Fund.

The crisis respected no national boundaries. A booming global economy focused on the quest for short-term profits was proving itself incapable of responding to increasingly urgent ecological and human crises; unable, for instance, to make the shift away from fossil fuels and toward sustainable energy sources; incapable, despite all the pledges and hand-wringing, of devoting the resources necessary to reverse the spread of HIV in Africa; unwilling to meet international commitments to reduce hunger or even address basic food security failures in Europe. It's difficult to say why the protest movement exploded when it did, since most of these social and environmental problems have been chronic for decades, but part of the credit, surely, has to go to globalization itself. When schools were underfunded or water supply was contaminated, it used to be blamed on the inept financial management or outright corruption of individual national governments. Now, thanks to a surge in cross-border information swapping, such problems were being recognized as the local effects of a particular global ideology, one enforced by national politicians but conceived of centrally by a handful of corporate interests and international institutions, including the World Trade Organization, the International Monetary Fund and the World Bank.

The irony of the media-imposed label "anti-globalization" is that we in this movement have been turning globalization into a lived reality, perhaps more so than even the most multinational of corporate executives or the most restless of jet-setters. At gatherings like the World Social Forum in Porto Alegre, at "counter-summits" during World Bank meetings and on communication networks like www.tao.ca and www.indymedia.org, globalization is not restricted to a narrow series of trade and tourism transactions. It is, instead, an intricate process of thousands of people tying their destinies together simply by sharing ideas and telling stories about how abstract economic theories affect their daily lives. This movement doesn't have leaders in the traditional sense— just people determined to learn, and to pass it on.

Like others who found themselves in this global web, I arrived equipped with only a limited understanding of neo-liberal economics, mostly how they related to young people growing up over-marketed and underemployed in North America and Europe. But like so many others, I have been globalized by this movement: I have received a crash course on what the market obsession has meant to landless farmers in Brazil, to teachers in Argentina, to fast-food workers in Italy, to coffee growers in Mexico, to shanty-town dwellers in South Africa, to telemarketers in France, to migrant tomato pickers in Florida, to union organizers in the Philippines, to homeless kids in Toronto, the city where I live.

This collection is a record of my own steep learning curve, one small part of a vast process of grassroots information sharing that has given swarms of people—people who are not trained as economists, international-trade lawyers or patent experts—the courage to participate in the debate about the future of the global economy. These columns, essays and speeches, written for *The Globe and Mail, The Guardian, The Los Angeles Times* and many other publications, were dashed off in hotel rooms late at night after protests in Washington and Mexico City, in Independent Media Centres, on way too many planes. (I'm on my second laptop, after the man in the cramped Air Canada economy seat in front of me pressed Recline, and I heard a terrible crunching sound.) They contain the most damning arguments and facts I could get my hands on to use in debates with neo-liberal economists, as well as the most moving experiences I had on the streets with fellow activists. Sometimes they represent hurried attempts to assimilate information that had arrived in my inbox only hours earlier, or to counter a new misinformation campaign attacking the nature and goals of the protests. Some of the essays, especially the speeches, have not been published before.

Why collect these ragtag writings into a book? In part because a few months into George W. Bush's "war on terrorism", a realization set in that something had ended. Some politicians (particularly those who have had their policies closely scrutinized by protestors) rushed to declare that what had ended was the movement itself: the concerns it raised about globalization's failures are frivolous, they claimed, even fodder for "the enemy." In fact, the escalation of military force and repression over the past year has provoked the largest protests yet on the streets of Rome, London, Barcelona and Buenos Aires. It has also inspired many activists, who had previously registered only symbolic dissent outside of summits, to take concrete actions to de-escalate the violence. These actions have included serving as "human shields" during the standoff at the Church of the Nativity in Bethlehem, as well as attempting to block illegal deportations of refugees at European and Australian detention centres. But as the movement entered this challenging new stage, I realized I had been witness to something extraordinary: the precise and thrilling moment when the rabble of the real world crashed the experts-only club where our collective fate is determined. So this is a record not of a conclusion but of that momentous beginning, a period bookended in North America by the joyous explosion on the streets of Seattle and catapulted to a new chapter by the unimaginable destruction on September 11.

—

Something else compelled me to pull together these articles. A few months ago, while riffling through my column clippings searching for a lost statistic, I noticed a couple of recurring themes and images. The first was the fence. The image came up again and again: barriers separating people from previously public resources, locking them away from much needed land and water, restricting their ability to move across borders, to express political dissent, to demonstrate on public streets, even keeping politicians from enacting policies that make sense for the people who elected them.

Some of these fences are hard to see, but they exist all the same. A virtual fence goes up around schools in Zambia when an education "user fee" is introduced on the advice of the World Bank, putting classes out of the reach of millions of people. A fence goes up around the family farm in Canada when government policies turn small-scale agriculture into a luxury item, unaffordable in a landscape of tumbling commodity prices and factory farms. There is a real if invisible fence that goes up around clean water in Soweto when prices skyrocket owing to privatization, and residents are forced to turn to contaminated sources. And there is a fence that goes up around the very idea of democracy when Argentina is told it won't get an International Monetary Fund loan unless it further reduces social spending, privatizes more resources and eliminates supports to local industries, all in the midst of an economic crisis deepened by those very policies. These fences, of course, are as old as colonialism. "Such usurious operations put bars around free nations," Eduardo Galeano wrote in *Open Veins of Latin America*. He was referring to the terms of a British loan to Argentina in 1824.

Fences have always been a part of capitalism, the only way to protect property from would-be bandits, but the double standards propping up these fences have, of late, become increasingly blatant. Expropriation of corporate holdings may be the greatest sin any socialist government can commit in the eyes of the international financial markets (just ask Venezuela's Hugo Chavez or Cuba's Fidel Castro). But the asset protection guaranteed to companies under free trade deals did not extend to the Argentine citizens who deposited their life savings in Citibank, Scotiabank and HSBC accounts and now find that most of their money has simply disappeared. Neither did the market's reverence for private wealth embrace the U.S. employees of Enron, who found that they had been "locked out" of their privatized retirement portfolios, unable to sell even as Enron executives were frantically cashing in their own stocks.

Meanwhile, some very necessary fences are under attack: in the rush to privatization, the barriers that once existed between many public and private spaces—keeping advertisements out of schools, for instance, profit-making interests out of health care, or news outlets from acting purely as promotional vehicles for their owners' other holdings—have nearly all been levelled. Every protected public space has been cracked open, only to be re-enclosed by the market.

Another public-interest barrier under serious threat is the one separating genetically modified crops from crops that have not yet been altered. The seed giants have done such a remarkably poor job of preventing their tampered seeds from blowing into neighbouring fields, taking root, and cross-pollinating, that in many parts of the world, eating GMO-free is no longer even an option—the entire food supply has been contaminated. The fences that protect the public interest seem to be fast disappearing, while the ones that restrict our liberties keep multiplying.

When I first noticed that the image of the fence kept coming up in discussion, debates and in my own writing, it seemed significant to me. After all, the past decade of economic integration has been fuelled by promises of barriers coming down, of increased mobility and greater freedom. And yet twelve years after the celebrated collapse of the Berlin Wall, we are surrounded by fences yet again, cut off—from one another, from the earth and from our own ability to imagine that change is possible. The economic process that goes by the benign euphemism "globalization" now reaches into every aspect of life, transforming every activity and natural resource into a measured and owned commodity. As the Hong Kong–based labour researcher Gerard Greenfield points out, the current stage of capitalism is not simply about trade in the traditional sense of selling more products across borders. It is also about feeding the market's insatiable need for growth by redefining as "products" entire sectors that were previously considered part of "the commons" and not for sale. The invading of the public by the private has reached into categories such as health and education, of course, but also ideas, genes, seeds, now purchased, patented and fenced off, as well as traditional aboriginal remedies, plants, water and even human stem cells. With copyright now the U.S.'s single largest export (more than manufactured goods or arms), international trade law must be understood not only as taking down selective barriers to trade but more accurately as a process that systematically puts up new barriers—around knowledge, technology and newly privatized resources. These Trade Related Intellectual Property Rights are what prevent farmers from replanting their Monsanto patented seeds and make it illegal for poor countries to manufacture cheaper generic drugs to get to their needy populations.

Globalization is now on trial because on the other side of all these virtual fences are real people, shut out of schools, hospitals, workplaces, their own farms, homes and communities. Mass privatization and deregulation have bred armies of locked-out people, whose services are no longer needed, whose lifestyles are written off as "backward," whose basic needs go unmet. These fences of social exclusion can discard an entire industry, and they can also write off an entire country, as has happened to Argentina. In the case of Africa, essentially an entire continent can find itself exiled to the global shadow world, off the map and off the news, appearing only during wartime when its citizens are looked on with suspicion as potential militia members, would-be terrorists or anti-American fanatics.

In fact, remarkably few of globalization's fenced-out people turn to violence. Most simply move: from countryside to city, from country to country. And that's when they come face to face with distinctly unvirtual fences, the ones made of chain link and razor wire, reinforced with concrete and guarded with machine guns. Whenever I hear the phrase "free trade," I can't help picturing the caged factories I visited in the Philippines and Indonesia that are all surrounded by gates, watchtowers and soldiers—to keep the highly subsidized products from leaking out and the union organizers from getting in. I think, too, about a recent trip to the South Australian desert where I visited the infamous Woomera detention centre. Located five hundred kilometres from the nearest city, Woomera is a former military base that has been converted into a privatized refugee holding pen, owned by a subsidiary of the U.S. security firm Wackenhut. At Woomera, hundreds of Afghan and Iraqi refugees, fleeing oppression and dictatorship in their own countries, are so desperate for the world to see what is going on behind the fence that they stage hunger strikes, jump off the roofs of their barracks, drink shampoo and sew their mouths shut.

These days, newspapers are filled with gruesome accounts of asylum seekers attempting to make it across national borders by hiding themselves among the products that enjoy so much more mobility than they do. In December 2001, the bodies of eight Romanian refugees, including two children, were discovered in a cargo container filled with office furniture; they had asphyxiated during the long journey at sea. The same year, the dead bodies of two more refugees were discovered in Eau Claire, Wisconsin, in a shipment of bathroom fixtures. The year before, fifty-four Chinese refugees from Fujian province suffocated in the back of a delivery truck in Dover, England.

All these fences are connected: the real ones, made of steel and razor wire, are needed to enforce the virtual ones, the ones that put resources and wealth out of the hands of so many. It simply isn't possible to lock away this much of our collective wealth without an accompanying strategy to control popular unrest and mobility. Security firms do their biggest business in the cities where the gap between rich and poor is greatest—Johannesburg, São Paulo, New Delhi—selling iron gates, armoured cars, elaborate alarm systems and renting out armies of private guards. Brazilians, for instance, spend US$4.5 billion a year on private security, and the country's 400,000 armed rent-a-cops outnumber actual police officers by almost four to one. In deeply divided South Africa, annual spending on private security has reached US$1.6 billion, more than three times what the government spends each year on affordable housing. It now seems that these gated compounds protecting the haves from the have-nots are microcosms of what is fast becoming a global security state—not a global village intent on lowering walls and barriers, as we were promised, but a network of fortresses connected by highly militarized trade corridors.

If this picture seems extreme, it may only be because most of us in the West rarely see the fences and the artillery. The gated factories and refugee detention centres remain tucked away in remote places, less able to pose a direct challenge to the seductive rhetoric of the borderless world. But over the past few years, some fences have intruded into full view—often, fittingly, during the summits where this brutal model of globalization is advanced. It is now taken for granted that if world leaders want to get together to discuss a new trade deal, they will need to build a modern-day fortress to protect themselves from public rage, complete with armoured tanks, tear gas, water cannons and attack dogs. When Quebec City hosted the Summit of the Americas in April 2001, the Canadian government took the unprecedented step of building a cage around, not just the conference centre, but the downtown core, forcing residents to show official documentation to get to their homes and workplaces. Another popular strategy is to hold the summits in inaccessible locations: the 2002 G8 meeting was held deep in the Canadian Rocky Mountains, and the 2001 WTO meeting took place in the repressive Gulf State of Qatar, where the emir bans political protests. The "war on terrorism" has become yet another fence to hide behind, used by summit organizers to explain why public shows of dissent just won't be possible this time around or, worse, to draw threatening parallels between legitimate protesters and terrorists bent on destruction.

But what are reported as menacing confrontations are often joyous events, as much experiments in alternative ways of organizing societies as criticisms of existing models. The first time I participated in one of these counter-summits, I remember having the distinct feeling that some sort of political portal was opening up—a gateway, a window, "a crack in history," to use Subcomandante Marcos's beautiful phrase. This opening had little to do with the broken window at the local McDonald's, the image so favoured by television cameras; it was something else: a sense of possibility, a blast of fresh air, oxygen rushing to the brain. These protests—which are actually week-long marathons of intense education on global politics, late-night strategy sessions in six-way simultaneous translation, festivals of music and street theatre—are like stepping into a parallel universe. Overnight, the site is transformed into a kind of alternative global city where urgency replaces resignation, corporate logos need armed guards, people usurp cars, art is everywhere, strangers talk to each other, and the prospect of a radical change in political course does not seem like an odd and anachronistic idea but the most logical thought in the world.

Even the heavy-handed security measures have been co-opted by activists into part of the message: the fences that surround the summits become metaphors for an economic model that exiles billions to poverty and exclusion. Confrontations are staged at the fence—but not only the ones involving sticks and bricks: tear-gas canisters have been flicked back with hockey sticks, water cannons have been irreverently challenged with toy water pistols and buzzing helicopters mocked with swarms of paper airplanes. During the Summit of the Americas in Quebec City, a group of activists built a medieval-style wooden catapult, wheeled it up to the three-metre-high fence that enclosed the downtown and lofted teddy bears over the top. In Prague, during a meeting of the World Bank and the International Monetary Fund, the Italian direct-action group Tute Bianche decided not to confront the black-clad riot police dressed in similarly threatening ski masks and bandanas; instead, they marched to the police line in white jumpsuits stuffed with rubber tires and Styrofoam padding. In a standoff between Darth Vader and an army of Michelin Men, the police couldn't win. Meanwhile, in another part of the city, the steep hillside leading up to the conference centre was scaled by a band of "pink fairies" dressed in burlesque wigs, silver-and-pink evening wear and platform shoes. These activists are quite serious in their desire to disrupt the current economic order, but their tactics reflect a dogged refusal to engage in classic power struggles: their goal, which I began to explore in the final pieces in this book, is not to take power for themselves but to challenge power centralization on principle.

Other kinds of windows are opening as well, quiet conspiracies to reclaim privatized spaces and assets for public use. Maybe it's students kicking ads out of their classrooms, or swapping music on-line, or setting up independent media centres with free software. Maybe it's Thai peasants planting organic vegetables on over-irrigated golf courses, or landless farmers in Brazil cutting down fences around unused lands and turning them into farming co-operatives. Maybe it's Bolivian workers reversing the privatization of their water supply, or South African township residents reconnecting their neighbours' electricity under the slogan Power to the People. And once reclaimed, these spaces are also being remade. In neighbourhood assemblies, at city councils, in independent media centres, in community-run forests and farms, a new culture of vibrant direct democracy is emerging, one that is fuelled and strengthened by direct participation, not dampened and discouraged by passive spectatorship.

Despite all the attempts at privatization, it turns out that there are some things that don't want to be owned. Music, water, seeds, electricity, ideas—they keep bursting out of the confines erected around them. They have a natural resistance to enclosure, a tendency to escape, to cross-pollinate, to flow through fences, and flee out open windows.

As I write this, it's not clear what will emerge from these liberated spaces, or if what emerges will be hardy enough to withstand the mounting attacks from the police and military, as the line between terrorist and activist is deliberately blurred. The question of what comes next preoccupies me, as it does everyone else who has been part of building this international movement. But this book is not an attempt to answer that question. It simply offers a view into the early life of the movement that exploded in Seattle and has evolved through the events of September 11 and its aftermath. I decided not to rewrite these articles, beyond a few very slight changes, usually indicated by square brackets— a reference explained, an argument expanded. They are presented here (more or less in chronological order) for what they are: postcards from dramatic moments in time, a record of the first chapter in a very old and recurring story, the one about people pushing up against the barriers that try to contain them, opening up windows, breathing deeply, tasting freedom.

I

WINDOWS OF DISSENT

[In which activists take down the first fences— on the streets and in their minds]

WINDOWS OF DISSENT

[In which activists take down the first fences—
on the streets and in their minds]

Seattle
The coming-out party of a movement

December 1999

"Who are these people?" That is the question being asked across the United States this week, on radio call-in shows, on editorial pages and, most of all, in the hallways of the World Trade Organization meeting in Seattle.

Until very recently, trade negotiations were genteel, experts-only affairs. There weren't protesters outside, let alone protesters dressed as giant sea turtles. But this week's WTO meeting is anything but genteel: a state of emergency has been declared in Seattle, the streets look like a war zone and the negotiations have collapsed.

There are plenty of theories floating around about the mysterious identities of the fifty thousand activists in Seattle. Some claim they are wannabe radicals with sixties envy. Or anarchists bent only on destruction. Or Luddites fighting against a tide of globalization that has already swamped them. Michael Moore, the director of the WTO, describes his opponents as nothing more than selfish pro-tectionists determined to hurt the world's poor.

Some confusion about the protesters' political goals is understandable. This is the first political movement born of the chaotic pathways of the Internet. Within its ranks, there is no top-down hierarchy ready to explain the master plan, no universally recognized leaders giving easy sound bites, and nobody knows what is going to happen next.

But one thing is certain: the protesters in Seattle are not anti-globalization; they have been bitten by the globalization bug as surely as the trade lawyers inside the official meetings. Rather, if this new movement is "anti" anything, it is anti-corporate, opposing the logic that what's good for business—less regulation, more mobility, more access—will trickle down into good news for everybody else.

The movement's roots are in campaigns that challenge this logic by focusing on the dismal human rights, labour and ecological records of a handful of multinational companies. Many of the young people on the streets of Seattle this week cut their activist teeth campaigning against Nike's sweatshops, or Royal Dutch/Shell's human rights record in the Niger Delta, or Monsanto's re-engineering of the global food supply. Over the past three years, these individual corporations have become symbols of the failings of the global economy, ultimately providing activists with name-brand entry points to the arcane world of the WTO.

By focusing on global corporations and their impact around the world, this activist network is fast becoming the most internationally minded, globally linked movement ever seen. There are no more faceless Mexicans or Chinese workers stealing "our" jobs, in part because those workers' representatives are now on the same e-mail lists and at the same conferences as the Western activists, and many even travelled to Seattle to join the demonstrations this week. When protesters shout about the evils of globalization, most are not calling for a return to narrow nationalism but for the borders of globalization to be expanded, for trade to be linked to labour rights, environmental protection and democracy.

This is what sets the young protesters in Seattle apart from their sixties predecessors. In the age of Woodstock, refusing to play by state and school rules was regarded as a political act in itself. Now, opponents of the WTO—even many who call themselves anarchists—are outraged about a *lack* of rules being applied to corporations, as well as the flagrant double standards in the application of existing rules in rich or poor countries.

They came to Seattle because they found out that WTO tribunals were overturning environmental laws protecting endangered species because the laws, apparently, were unfair trade barriers. Or they learned that France's decision to ban hormone-laced beef was deemed by the WTO to be unacceptable interference with the free market. What is on trial in Seattle is not trade or globalization but the global attack on the right of citizens to set rules that protect people and the planet.

Everyone, of course, claims to be all for rules, from President Clinton to Microsoft's chairman, Bill Gates. In an odd turn of events, the need for "rules-based trade" has become the mantra of the era of deregulation. But the WTO has consistently sought to sever trade, quite unnaturally, from everything and everyone affected by it: workers, the environment, culture. This is why President Clinton's suggestion yesterday that the rift between the protesters and the delegates can be smoothed over with small compromises and consultation is so misguided.

The faceoff is not between globalizers and protectionists but between two radically different visions of globalization. One has had a monopoly for the past ten years. The other just had its coming-out party.

Washington, D.C.
Capitalism comes out of the closet

April 2000

BEFORE

My friend Mez is getting on a bus to Washington, D.C., on Saturday. I asked him why. He said with great intensity, "Look, I missed Seattle. There's no way I'm missing Washington."

I'd heard people speak with that kind of unrestrained longing before, but the object of their affection was usually a muddy music festival or a short-run New York play like *The Vagina Monologues.* I've never heard anyone talk that way about a political protest. Especially not a protest against groaner bureaucracies like the World Bank and the International Monetary Fund. And certainly not when they are being called on the carpet for nothing sexier than a decades-old loan policy called "structural adjustment."

And yet there they are: university students and artists and wage-free anarchists and lunch-box steelworkers, piling onto buses from all corners of the continent. Stuffed in their pockets and shoulder bags are fact sheets about the ratio of spending on health care to debt repayment in Mozambique (two and a half times more for debt) and the number of people worldwide living without electricity (two billion).

Four months ago, this same coalition of environmental, labour and anarchist groups brought a World Trade Organization meeting to a standstill. In Seattle, an impressive range of single-issue campaigns—some focused on controversial corporations such as Nike or Shell, some on dictatorships such as Burma—broadened their focus to a more structural critique of the regulatory bodies playing referee in a global race to the bottom.

Caught off guard by the strength and organization of the opposition, the proponents of accelerated free trade immediately went on the offensive, attacking the protesters as enemies of the poor. Most memorably, *The Economist* put a picture of a starving Indian child on its cover and claimed that this was who was really being hurt by the protests. WTO chief Michael Moore got all choked up: "To those who would argue that we should stop our work, I say: Tell that to the poor, to the marginalized around the world who are looking to us to help them."

The recasting of the WTO, and of global capitalism itself, as a tragically misunderstood poverty elimination program is the single most off-putting legacy of the Battle in Seattle. To hear the line coming out of Geneva, barrier-free trade is a giant philanthropic plan, and multinational corporations are using their soaring shareholder returns and executive salaries only to disguise their real intentions: to heal the world's sick, to raise the minimum wage and to save the trees.

But nothing does a better job of giving the lie to this specious equation of humanitarian goals with deregulated trade than the track record of the World Bank and the IMF, who have exacerbated world poverty with a zealous and near-mystical faith in trickle-down economics.

The World Bank has lent money to the poorest and most desperate nations to build economies based on foreign-owned megaprojects, cash-crop farming, low-wage export-driven manufacturing and speculative finance. These projects have been a boon to multinational mining, textile, and agribusiness companies around the world, but in many countries they have also led to environmental devastation, mass migration to urban centres, currency crashes and dead-end sweatshop jobs.

Which is where the World Bank and IMF come in with their infamous bailouts, always with more conditions attached. In Haiti, it was a frozen minimum wage, in Thailand the elimination of restrictions on foreign ownership, in Mexico a hike in university fees was urged. And when these latest austerity measures fail once again to lead to sustainable economic growth, these countries are still on the hook for their layers of debts.

As international attention turns to the World Bank and IMF this weekend, it will go a long way toward countering the argument that the protesters in Seattle were greedy North American protectionists, determined to keep the fruits of the economic boom to themselves. When union members and environmentalists took to the streets to complain about WTO interference in environmental and labour regulation, they weren't trying to impose "our" standards on the developing world. They were playing catch-up with a movement for self-determination that began in the southern nations of the world, where the words "World Bank" are spat, not said, and where "IMF" is parodied on protest signs as short for "I M Fired."

After Seattle, it was relatively easy for the World Trade Organization to win the spin wars. So few people had even heard of the WTO before the protests that the organization's claims were left mostly unchallenged. But the World Bank and the IMF are a different story: prod them even a little bit and all the skeletons come tumbling out of the closet. Usually the skeletons can only be seen in poor countries— crumbling schools and hospitals, farmers thrown off their land, overcrowded cities, toxic water systems. But this weekend all that changes; the skeletons are following the bankers home to head office, in Washington, D.C.

AFTER

Okay, I admit it: I slept in.

I went to Washington for the protests against the World Bank and the International Monetary Fund, but when my cellphone rang at some ungodly hour with word that the new plan was to meet at 4 A.M. on Monday, I just couldn't do it.

"Okay, meet you there," I mumbled, scribbling street intersections with a pen that had run out of ink. There was absolutely no way. Bone-tired after thirteen hours on the streets the day before, I decided to catch up with the demos at a more civilized hour. And so, it seems, did a few thousand other people, allowing the World Bank delegates, bussed in before dawn, to get to their meeting in bleary-eyed peace.

"A defeat!" many of the newspapers pronounced, eager to put this outbreak of messy democracy behind them.

Canadian-expat-in-Washington David Frum couldn't get to his computer fast enough, declaring the protests "a flop," "a disaster" and, for good measure, "a flat soufflé." In Frum's estimation, the activists were so discouraged by their inability to shut down the IMF meeting on Sunday that they took to their beds the next day rather than brave the rainy streets.

It's true it was tough to drag butt out of bed on Monday, but not because of the rain or the cops. It was tough because by then so much had already been accomplished in a single week of protests. Shutting down a meeting is good activist bragging rights, no doubt, but the real victories happen around those dramatic moments.

The first sign of victory came in the weeks before the protest, with a rush among former World Bank and IMF officials to come out on the side of the critics and renounce their former employers. Most notably, former World Bank chief economist Joseph Stiglitz said the IMF was in desperate need of a large dose of democracy and transparency.

Next, a corporation gave in. The protest organizers had announced that they would take their calls for "fair trade" as opposed to "free trade" to the doorstep of the Starbucks coffee chain, demanding that it sell coffee grown by farmers who are paid a living wage. Last week, only four days before the planned protest, Starbucks announced it would carry a line of fair-trade-certified coffee—not an earth-shattering victory but a sign of the times at least.

And, finally, the protesters defined the terms of debate. Before the giant papier-mâché puppets were dry, the failures of many World Bank–financed megaprojects and IMF bailouts were outlined in newspapers and radio talk shows. More than that, the critique of "capitalism" just saw a comeback of Santana-like proportions.

The radical anarchist contingent the Black Bloc renamed itself the Anti-Capitalist Bloc. College students wrote in chalk on the sidewalks: "If you think the IMF and World Bank are scary, wait until you hear about Capitalism." The frat boys at American University responded with their own slogans, written on placards and hung in their windows: "Capitalism brought you prosperity. Embrace it!" Even the Sunday pundits on CNN started saying the word "capitalism" instead of just "the economy." And the word makes not one but two appearances on the cover of yesterday's *New York Times*. After more than a decade of unchecked triumphalism, capitalism (as opposed to euphemisms such as "globalization," "corporate rule" or "the growing gap between rich and poor") has re-emerged as a legitimate subject of public debate. This kind of impact is so significant that it makes the disruption of a routine World Bank meeting seem almost beside the point. The agenda of the World Bank meeting, and the press conference that followed, was hijacked utterly. The usual talk of deregulation, privatization and the need to "discipline" Third World markets was supplanted by commitments to speed up debt relief for impoverished nations and spend "unlimited" sums on the African AIDS crisis.

Of course, this is only the beginning of a long process. But if there is a lesson of Washington, it is that a barricade can be stormed in spirit, as well as in body. Monday's sleep-in wasn't the nap of the defeated, it was the well-deserved rest of the victorious.

What's Next?

The movement against global corporatism doesn't need to sign a ten-point plan to be effective

July 2000

"This conference is not like other conferences."

That's what all the speakers at "Re-Imagining Politics and Society" were told before we arrived at New York's Riverside Church. When we addressed the delegates (there were about a thousand over three days in May), we were to try to solve a very specific problem: the lack of "unity of vision and strategy" guiding the movement against global corporatism.

This was a very serious problem, we were advised. The young activists who went to Seattle to shut down the World Trade Organization and to Washington, D.C., to protest the World Bank and the International Monetary Fund had been getting hammered in the press as tree-wearing, lamb-costumed, drumbeating bubble brains. Our mission, according to the conference organizers at the Foundation for Ethics and Meaning, was to whip that chaos on the streets into some kind of structured, media-friendly shape. This wasn't just another talk shop. We were going to "give birth to a unified movement for holistic social, economic and political change."

As I slipped in and out of lecture rooms, soaking up the vision offered by Arianna Huffington, Michael Lerner, David

Korten, Cornel West and dozens of others, I was struck by the futility of this entire well-meaning exercise. Even if we did manage to come up with a ten-point plan—brilliant in its clarity, elegant in its coherence, unified in its outlook— to whom, exactly, would we hand down these commandments? The anti-corporate protest movement that came to world attention on the streets of Seattle last November is not united by a political party or a national network with a head office, annual elections and subordinate cells and locals. It is shaped by the ideas of individual organizers and intellectuals but doesn't defer to any of them as leaders. In this amorphous context, the ideas and plans being hatched at the Riverside Church weren't irrelevant exactly, they just weren't important in the way that was hoped. Rather than being adopted as activist policy, they were destined to be swept up and tossed around in the tidal wave of information—Web diaries, NGO manifestos, academic papers, homemade videos, cris de coeur—that the global anti-corporate network produces and consumes each and every day.

This is the flip side of the persistent criticism that the kids on the street lack clear leadership—they lack clear followers too. To those searching for copies of efforts from the sixties, this absence makes the anti-corporate movement appear infuriatingly impassive: evidently, these people are so disorganized they can't even get it together to respond to perfectly well-organized efforts to organize them. These are MTV-weaned activists, you can practically hear the old guard saying: scattered, nonlinear, unfocused.

It's easy to be taken in by these critiques. If there is one thing that the left and right agree on, it is the value of a clear, well-structured ideological argument. But maybe it's not quite so simple. Maybe the protests in Seattle and Washington, D.C., look unfocused because they were not demonstrations of one movement at all but rather convergences of many smaller ones, each with its sights trained on a specific multinational corporation (like Nike), a particular industry (like agribusiness) or a new trade initiative (like the Free Trade Area of the Americas). These smaller, targeted movements are clearly part of a common cause: they share a belief that the disparate problems they are wrestling with all derive from corporate-driven globalization, an agenda that is concentrating power and wealth into fewer and fewer hands. Of course, there are disagreements—about the role of the nation-state, about whether capitalism is redeemable, about the speed with which change should occur. But within most of these miniature movements, there is an emerging consensus that decentralizing power and building community-based decision-making potential— whether through unions, neighbourhoods, farms, villages, anarchist collectives or aboriginal self-government—is essential to countering the might of multinational corporations.

Despite this common ground, these campaigns have not coalesced into a single movement. Rather, they are intricately and tightly linked to one another, much as "hotlinks" connect their Web sites on the Internet. This analogy is more than coincidental and is in fact key to understanding the changing nature of political organizing. Although many have observed that the recent mass protests would have been impossible without the Internet, what has been overlooked is how the communication technology that facilitates these campaigns is shaping the movement in its own Web-like image. Thanks to the Net, mobilizations occur with sparse bureaucracy and minimal hierarchy; forced consensus and laboured manifestos are fading into the background, replaced instead by a culture of constant, loosely structured and sometimes compulsive information swapping.

What emerged on the streets of Seattle and Washington was an activist model that mirrors the organic, decentralized, interlinked pathways of the Internet—the Internet come to life.

The Washington-based research centre TeleGeography has taken it upon itself to map out the architecture of the Internet as if it were the solar system. Recently, TeleGeography pronounced that the Internet is not one giant web but a network of "hubs and spokes." The hubs are the centres of activity, the spokes the links to other centres, which are autonomous but interconnected.

It seems like a perfect description of the protests in Seattle and Washington, D.C. These mass convergences were activist hubs, made up of hundreds, possibly thousands, of autonomous spokes. During the demonstrations, the spokes took the form of "affinity groups" of between five and twenty protesters, each of which elected a spokesperson to represent them at regular "spokescouncil" meetings. Although the affinity groups agreed to abide by a set of non-violence principles, they also functioned as discrete units, with the power to make their own strategic decisions. At some rallies, activists carry actual cloth webs to symbolize their movement. When it's time for a meeting, they lay the web on the ground, call out "all spokes on the web" and the structure becomes a street-level boardroom.

In the four years before the Seattle and Washington protests, similar hub events had converged outside World Trade Organization, G7 and Asia Pacific Economic Co-operation summits in Auckland, Vancouver, Manila, Birmingham, London, Geneva, Kuala Lumpur and Cologne. Each of these mass protests was organized according to principles of co-ordinated decentralization. Rather than present a coherent front, small units of activists surrounded their target from all directions. And rather than build elaborate national or international bureaucracies, they threw up temporary structures: empty buildings were turned into "convergence centres," and independent media producers assembled impromptu activist news centres. The ad hoc coalitions behind these demonstrations frequently named themselves after the date of the planned event: J18, N30, A16 and, for the upcoming IMF meeting in Prague on September 26, S26. When these events are over, they leave virtually no trace behind, save for an archived Web site.

All this talk of radical decentralization can conceal a very real hierarchy based on who owns, understands and controls the computer networks linking the activists to one another. This is what Jesse Hirsh, one of the founders of the anarchist computer network Tao Communications, calls "a geek adhocracy."

The hubs and spokes model is more than a tactic used at protests; the protests are themselves made up of "coalitions of coalitions," to borrow a phrase from Kevin Danaher of Global Exchange. Each anti-corporate campaign is made up of many groups, mostly NGOs, labour unions, students and anarchists. They use the Internet, as well as more traditional organizing tools, to do everything from cataloguing the latest transgressions of the World Bank to bombarding Shell Oil with faxes and e-mails, to distributing ready-to-download anti-sweatshop leaflets for protests at Nike Town. The groups remain autonomous, but their international co-ordination is deft and, to their targets, frequently devastating.

The charge that the anti-corporate movement lacks "vision" falls apart when looked at in the context of these campaigns. It's true that the mass protests in Seattle and D.C. were a hodgepodge of slogans and causes, that to a casual observer it was hard to decode the connections between the treatment of U.S. death row inmate Mumia Abu-Jamal and the fate of the sea turtles. But in trying to find coherence in these large-scale shows of strength, the critics are confusing the outward demonstrations of the movement with the thing itself—missing the forest for the people dressed as trees. This movement *is* its spokes, and in the spokes there is no shortage of vision.

The student anti-sweatshop movement, for instance, has rapidly moved from simply criticizing companies and campus administrators to drafting alternative codes of conduct and building a quasi-regulatory body, the Worker Rights Consortium in partnership with labour activists in the global south. The movement against genetically engineered and modified foods has leaped from one policy victory to the next, first getting many genetically modified foods removed from the shelves of British supermarkets, then getting labelling laws passed in Europe, then making enormous strides with the Montreal Protocol on Biosafety. Meanwhile, opponents of the World Bank's and IMF's export-led development models have produced bookshelves' worth of resources on community-based development models, land reform, debt cancellation and self-government principles. Critics of the oil and mining industries are similarly overflowing with ideas for sustainable energy and responsible resource extraction—though they rarely get the chance to put their visions into practice.

The fact that these campaigns are so decentralized does not mean they are incoherent. Rather, decentralization is a reasonable, even ingenious adaptation both to pre-existing fragmentation within progressive networks and to changes in the broader culture. It is a by-product of the explosion of NGOs, which, since the Rio Summit in 1992, have been gaining power and prominence. There are so many NGOs involved in anti-corporate campaigns that nothing but the hubs-and-spokes model could possibly accommodate all their different styles, tactics and goals. Like the Internet itself, both the NGO and the affinity group networks are infinitely expandable systems. If somebody feels that he or she doesn't quite fit into one of the thirty thousand or so NGOs or thousands of affinity groups out there, she can just start her own and link up. Once involved, no one has to give up individuality to the larger structure; as with all things on-line, we are free to dip in and out, take what we want and delete what we don't. It seems, at times, to be a surfer's approach to activism—reflecting the Internet's paradoxical culture of extreme narcissism coupled with an intense desire for community and connection.

But while the movement's Web-like structure is, in part, a reflection of Internet-based organizing, it is also a response to the very political realities that sparked the protests in the first place: the utter failure of traditional party politics. All over the world, citizens have worked to elect social democratic and workers' parties, only to watch them plead impotence in the face of market forces and IMF dictates. In these conditions, modern activists are not so naive as to believe change will come from the ballot box. That's why they are more interested in challenging the mechanisms that make democracy toothless, like corporate financing of election campaigns or the WTO's ability to override national sovereignty. The most controversial of these mechanisms have been the IMF's structural adjustment policies, which are overt in their demands for governments to cut social spending and privatize resources in exchange for loans.

One of the great strengths of this model of laissez-faire organizing is that it has proven extraordinarily difficult to control, largely because it is so different from the organizing principles of the institutions and corporations it targets. It responds to corporate concentration with fragmentation, to globalization with its own kind of localization, to power consolidation with radical power dispersal.

Joshua Karliner of the Transnational Resource and Action Center calls this system "an unintentionally brilliant response to globalization." And because it was unintentional, we still lack even the vocabulary to describe it, which may be why a rather amusing metaphor industry has evolved to fill the gap. I'm throwing my lot in with hubs and spokes, but Maude Barlow of the Council of Canadians says, "We are up against a boulder. We can't remove it, so we try to go underneath it, to go around it and over it." Britain's John Jordan, an activist with Reclaim the Streets, says transnationals "are like giant tankers, and we are like a school of fish. We can respond quickly; they can't." The U.S.-based Free Burma Coalition talks of a network of "spiders," spinning a web strong enough to tie down the most powerful multinationals. A U.S. military report about the Zapatista uprising in Chiapas, Mexico, even got in on the game. According to a study produced by RAND, a research institute that does contracts for the U.S. military, the Zapatistas were waging "a war of the flea" that, thanks to the Internet and the global NGO network, turned into a "war of the swarm." The military challenge of a war of the swarm, the researchers noted, is that it has no "central leadership or command structure; it is multiheaded, impossible to decapitate."

Of course, this multiheaded system has its weaknesses too, and they were on full display on the streets of Washington during the anti–World Bank/IMF protests. At around noon on April 16, the day of the largest protest, a spokescouncil meeting was convened for the affinity groups that were in the midst of blocking all the street intersections surrounding the headquarters of the World Bank and the IMF. The intersections had been blocked since 6 A.M., but the meeting delegates, the protesters had just learned, had slipped inside the police barricades before 5 A.M. With this new information, most of the spokespeople felt it was time to give up the intersections and join the official march at the Ellipse. The problem was that not everyone agreed: a handful of affinity groups wanted to see if they could block the delegates on their way out of their meetings.

The compromise the council came up with was telling. "Okay, everybody listen up," Kevin Danaher, one of the protest organizers, shouted into a megaphone. "Each intersection has autonomy. If the intersection wants to stay locked down, that's cool. If it wants to come to the Ellipse, that's cool too. It's up to you."

This was impeccably fair and democratic, but there was just one problem—it made absolutely no sense. Sealing off the access points had been a co-ordinated action. If some intersections now opened up and other rebel-camp intersections stayed occupied, delegates on their way out of the meeting could just hang a right instead of a left, and they would be home free. Which, of course, is precisely what happened.

As I watched clusters of protesters get up and wander off while others stayed seated, defiantly guarding, well, nothing, it struck me as an apt metaphor for the strengths and weaknesses of this nascent activist network. There is no question that the communication culture that reigns on the Net is better at speed and volume than at synthesis. It is capable of getting tens of thousands of people to meet on the same street corner, placards in hand, but is far less adept at helping those same people to agree on what they are really asking for before they get to the barricades—or after they leave.

For this reason, an odd sort of anxiety has begun to set in after each demonstration: Was that it? When's the next one? Will it be as good, as big? To keep up the momentum, a culture of serial protesting is rapidly taking hold. My inbox is cluttered with entreaties to come to what promises to be "the next Seattle." There was Windsor and Detroit on June 4, 2000, for a "shutdown" of the Organization of American States, and Calgary a week later for the World Petroleum Congress; the Republican convention in Philadelphia in July and the Democratic convention in L.A. in August; the World Economic Forum's Asia Pacific Economic Summit on September 11 in Melbourne, followed shortly thereafter by anti-IMF demos on September 26 in Prague and then on to Quebec City for the Summit of the Americas in April 2001. Someone posted a message on the organizing e-mail list for the Washington demos: "Wherever they go, we shall be there! After this, see you in Prague!" But is this really what we want—a movement of meeting stalkers, following the trade bureaucrats as if they were the Grateful Dead?

The prospect is dangerous for several reasons. Far too much expectation is being placed on these protests: the organizers of the D.C. demo, for instance, announced they would literally "shut down" two $30 billion transnational institutions, at the same time as they attempted to convey sophisticated ideas about the fallacies of neo-liberal economics to the stock-happy public. They simply couldn't do it; no single demo could, and it's only going to get harder. Seattle's direct-action tactics worked because they took the police by surprise. That won't happen again. Police have now subscribed to all the e-mail lists. The city of Los Angeles has already put in a request for $4 million in new security gear and staffing costs to protect the city from the activist swarm.

In an attempt to build a stable political structure to advance the movement between protests, Danaher has begun to fundraise for a "permanent convergence centre" in Washington. The International Forum on Globalization, meanwhile, has been meeting since March in hopes of producing a two-hundred-page policy paper by the end of the year. According to IFG director Jerry Mander, it won't be a manifesto but a set of principles and priorities, an early attempt, as he puts it, at "defining a new architecture" for the global economy. [The paper was delayed many times and was still not available at the time of this book's publication.]

Like the conference organizers at the Riverside Church, however, these initiatives face an uphill battle. Most activists agree that the time has come to sit down and start discussing a positive agenda—but at whose table, and who gets to decide?

These questions came to a head at the end of May when Czech President Vaclav Havel offered to "mediate" talks between World Bank president James Wolfensohn and the protesters planning to disrupt the bank's September 26–28 meeting in Prague. There was no consensus among protest organizers about participating in the negotiations at Prague Castle, and more to the point, there was no process in place to make the decision: no mechanism to select acceptable members of an activist delegation (some suggested an Internet vote) and no agreed-upon set of goals to measure the benefits and pitfalls of taking part. If Havel had reached out to the groups specifically dealing with debt and structural adjustment, like Jubilee 2000 or 50 Years Is Enough, the proposal would have been dealt with in a straightforward manner. But because he approached the entire movement as if it was a single unit, he sent those organizing the demonstrations into weeks of internal strife.

Part of the problem is structural. Among most anarchists, who are doing a great deal of the grassroots organizing (and who got on-line way before the more established left), direct democracy, transparency and community self-determination are not lofty political goals, they are fundamental tenets governing their own organizations. Yet many of the key NGOs, though they may share the anarchists' ideas about democracy in theory, are themselves organized like traditional hierarchies. They are run by charismatic leaders and executive boards, while their members send them money and cheer from the sidelines.

So how do you extract coherence from a movement filled with anarchists, whose greatest tactical strength so far has been its similarity to a swarm of mosquitoes? Maybe, as with the Internet, the best approach is to learn to surf the structures that are emerging organically. Perhaps what is needed is not a single political party but better links among the affinity groups; perhaps rather than moving toward more centralization, what is needed is further radical decentralization.

When critics say that the protesters lack vision, they are really objecting to a lack of an overarching revolutionary philosophy—like Marxism, democratic socialism, deep ecology or social anarchy—that they all agree on. That is absolutely true, and for this we should be extraordinarily thankful. At the moment, the anti-corporate street activists are ringed by would-be leaders, eager for the opportunity to enlist activists as foot soldiers for their particular vision. At one end there is Michael Lerner and his conference at the

Riverside Church, waiting to welcome all that inchoate energy in Seattle and Washington inside the framework of his "Politics of Meaning." At the other, there is John Zerzan in Eugene, Oregon, who isn't interested in Lerner's call for "healing" but sees the rioting and property destruction as the first step toward the collapse of industrialization and a return to "anarcho-primitivism"—a pre-agrarian hunter-gatherer utopia. In between there are dozens of other visionaries, from the disciples of Murray Bookchin and his theory of social ecology, to certain sectarian Marxists who are convinced the revolution starts tomorrow, to devotees of Kalle Lasn, editor of *Adbusters,* and his watered-down version of revolution through "culture jamming." And then there is the unimaginative pragmatism coming from some union leaders who, before Seattle, were ready to tack social clauses onto existing trade agreements and call it a day.

It is to this young movement's credit that it has as yet fended off all these agendas and has rejected everyone's generously donated manifesto, holding out for an acceptably democratic, representative process to take its resistance to the next stage. Perhaps its true challenge is not finding a vision but rather resisting the urge to settle on one too quickly. If it succeeds in warding off the teams of visionaries-in-waiting, there will be some short-term public relations problems. Serial protesting will burn some people out. Street intersections will declare autonomy. And yes, young activists will offer themselves up like lambs—dressed, frequently enough, in actual lamb costumes—to *The New York Times* op-ed page for ridicule.

But so what? Already, this decentralized, multiheaded

swarm of a movement has succeeded in educating and radicalizing a generation of activists around the world. Before it signs on to anyone's ten-point plan, it deserves the chance to see if, out of its chaotic network of hubs and spokes, something new, something entirely its own, can emerge.

Los Angeles
X-raying the marriage of money and politics

August 2000

This speech was delivered in Los Angeles at the Shadow Convention, just blocks away from the Staples Center, where the Democratic National Convention was taking place. The Shadow Convention was a week-long conference to explore significant issues—such as campaign finance reform and the war on drugs—that the major U.S. political parties were ignoring at their conventions. This speech was part of a panel called "Challenging the Money Culture."

Exposing corporations—the way they have swallowed our public spaces, our ideas about rebellion and bought our politicians—is no longer just a pursuit for cultural critics and academics. It has become, in only a few short years, an international contact sport. All over the world, activists are saying, "Yes, we get it. We've read the books. We've been to the lectures. We've studied the octopus-like charts in *The Nation* that show Rupert Murdoch owns everything. And guess what? We're not just going to feel bad about it. We are going to do something about it."

Has anti-corporate activism brought corporate America to its knees? No. But it is not insignificant either. Just ask Nike. Or Microsoft. Or Shell Oil. Or Monsanto. Or Occidental Petroleum. Or the Gap. Ask Philip Morris. They'll tell you. Or rather they will have their newly appointed vice-president of corporate responsibility tell you.

We live in an era of the high commodity fetish, to borrow a phrase from Karl Marx. Soft drink and computer brands play the roles of deities in our culture. They are creating our most powerful iconography, they are the ones building our most utopian monuments, they are the ones articulating our experience back to us: not religions, not intellectuals, not poets, not politicians. They are all on the Nike payroll now.

In response, we are in the midst of the first stages of an organized political campaign to de-fetishize commodities, to say, no, that sneaker is *not,* in fact, a symbol of rebellion and transcendence. It's a piece of rubber and leather and somebody stitched the two together and I'll tell you how and how much she got paid for it and how many union organizers had to be fired to keep the price down. Commodity de-fetishization is about saying that that Mac computer has nothing to do with Martin Luther King Jr. but does have to do with an industry bent on building information cartels.

It is about recognizing that every piece of our high-gloss consumer culture comes from somewhere. It is about following the webs of contracted factories, shell-game subsidiaries and outsourced labour to find out where all the pieces are manufactured, under what conditions, which lobby groups wrote the rules of the game and which politicians were bought off along the way. In other words, it's about X-raying commodity culture, deconstructing the icons of the age of shopping and building real global connections—among workers, students, environmentalists—in the process. We are witnessing a new wave of investigative, name-naming activism: part Black Panther, part Black Bloc, part situationist, part slapstick, part Marxist, part marketing.

And we are seeing it all over L.A. this week. On Sunday, there was a protest at the Loews Hotel, the site of a bitter labour dispute between low-wage workers and management. The strikers chose this week for their rally because they wanted to draw attention to the fact that the CEO of Loews is a major contributor to Al Gore's campaign. They wanted to make two points: that the economic boom is being built on the back of low-wage workers, and that our politicians are looking the other way because they are kept men and women. Later that day there was a rally at the Gap. This rally also had two purposes. The first was to draw attention to the way the company has funded all those funky khakis commercials—by getting cut-rate deals on their production from sweatshop factories; the second was to draw the connection between campaign donations and corporate lobbying. "What is Gap Chairman Donald Fisher's favorite hobby?" the flyers asked. "Buying politicians," they answered, noting the company's generous donation to both George Bush and Bill Bradley. On Monday, the target was Gore's personal holdings in Occidental Petroleum, an oil company embroiled in a human rights dispute in Colombia where it plans to drill on U'wa land, despite the tribespeople's threat to commit mass suicide if their land is desecrated. [The company has since withdrawn from the project.]

I believe this convention will be remembered as the one

where the marriage of money and politics was definitively dragged out of the shadows—here at the Shadow Convention, and on the street with Billionaires for Bush (or Gore) who are symbolically gagging themselves with fake million-dollar bills. Ideas that only a handful of policy wonks used to care about—campaign finance reform, media concentration— have taken on a life of their own. They are floating back as street-theatre skits on Figueroa Street and astonishingly successful participatory media networks like Indymedia, which has taken over the sixth floor of this building, the Patriotic Hall.

With so much springing up in just a few years, how can we dare to be hopeless about the possibility for change in the future? Remember, the young people taking on corporate power on the streets are the very ones who had been written off as beyond redemption. This is the generation that grew up entirely under the marketing microscope. They were the ones with commercials in their classrooms; stalked on the Internet by voracious market researchers; with youth subcultures fully bought and sold; told that their greatest aspiration should be to become a dot-com millionaire at eighteen; and taught that rather than being a citizen they should learn "to be the CEO of Me Inc." or, in the catch phrase of the moment, "a Brand Called You." These people were supposed to have grape Fruitopia in their veins instead of blood, and Palm Pilots instead of brains.

And, sure, some do. But many are going in precisely the opposite direction. For this reason, if we are to build a broad-based movement that challenges the money culture, we need activism that functions on concrete policy levels. But it also has to go deeper, to address the cultural and human needs created by the commodification of identity itself. It is going to have to recognize the need for non-commodified experiences and to reawaken our desire for truly public spaces, and for the thrill of building something collectively. Maybe we should start asking ourselves whether the free software movement and Napster are part of this phenomenon. Maybe we have to start liberating more privatized spaces, as the travelling activist caravan Reclaim the Streets does, throwing wild parties in the middle of busy intersections just to remind people that streets were once civic spaces as well as commercial ones.

This reclaiming is already happening on many fronts. The commons is being reclaimed around the world: by media activists, by landless peasants occupying unused land, by farmers rejecting the patenting of plants and life forms.

And democracy is being reclaimed as well, by the people in this room and in the street outside. It doesn't want to be enclosed in the Staples Center, or penned in by the bankrupt logic of the two corporate parties. And here in Los Angeles, the activism that came to world attention in Seattle is bursting out of its own confines, transforming itself from a movement opposed to corporate power to one fighting for the liberation of democracy itself.

Prague
The alternative to capitalism isn't communism, it's decentralized power

September 2000

What seems to most enrage the delegates to the meeting of the World Bank and the International Monetary Fund in Prague this week is the idea that they even have to discuss the basic benefits of free-market globalization. That discussion was supposed to have stopped in 1989, when the Berlin Wall fell and history ended. Only here we all are—old people, young people, thousands of us—literally storming the barricades of their extremely important summit.

And as the delegates peer over the side of their ill-protected fortress at the crowds below, scanning signs that say "Capitalism Kills," they look terribly confused. Didn't these strange people get the memo? Don't they understand that we all already decided that free-market capitalism was the last, best system? Sure, it's not perfect, and everyone inside the meeting is awfully concerned about all those poor people and the environmental mess, but it's not as if there's a choice—is there?

For the longest time, it seemed as if there were only two political models: Western capitalism and Soviet communism. When the U.S.S.R. collapsed, that left only one alternative, or so it seemed. Institutions like the World Bank and IMF have been busily "adjusting" economies in Eastern Europe and Asia to help them get with the program: privatizing services, relaxing regulation of foreign corporations, weakening unions, building huge export industries.

All this is why it is so significant that yesterday's head-on attack against the ideology ruling the World Bank and the IMF happened here, in the Czech Republic. This is a country that has lived through both economic orthodoxies, where the Lenin busts have been replaced by Pepsi logos and McDonald's arches.

Many of the young Czechs I met this week say that their direct experience with communism and capitalism has taught them that the two systems have something in common: they both centralize power in the hands of a few, and they both treat people as if they are less than fully human. Where communism saw them only as potential producers, capitalism sees them only as potential consumers; where communism starved their beautiful capital, capitalism has overfed it, turning Prague into a Velvet Revolution theme park.

The experience of growing up disillusioned with both systems explains why so many of the activists behind this week's event call themselves anarchists, and why they feel an intuitive connection with peasant farmers or the urban poor in developing countries, fighting huge institutions and faceless bureaucracies like the IMF and World Bank.

What connects these issues is a critique not of who is in power—the state versus the multinationals—but of how power is distributed, and a belief that decision making is always more accountable when it's closer to the people who must live with the decisions. At its root is a rejection of "trust us" culture, no matter who is the expert of the moment. During the Velvet Revolution, the parents of many young activists in Prague successfully fought to change who was in power in their country. Their children, sensing that it still isn't the Czech people, are now part of a global movement challenging the mechanisms of power centralization itself.

At a globalization conference in the lead-up to the Prague meeting, Indian physicist Vandana Shiva explained mass rejection of World Bank projects as less a dispute over a particular dam or social program and more a fight for local democracy and self-government. "The history of the World Bank," she said, has been "to take power away from communities, give it to a central government, then give it to the corporations through privatization."

The young anarchists in the crowd nodded. She sounded just like them.

Toronto
Anti-poverty activism and the violence debate

June 2000

How do you organize a riot? That is an important question right now for John Clarke, the most visible member of the Ontario Coalition Against Poverty. Last week OCAP held a rally to protest the spiralling homelessness that has led to twenty-two street deaths in seven months. After it turned into a pitched battle with charging horses and riot police confronted by bricks and boards, Clarke was instantly singled out as a Machiavellian puppeteer, pulling the strings of a limp, witless rent-a-mob.

Several unions threatened to withdraw their funding from the anti-poverty group, and Clarke himself faces criminal charges for allegedly inciting a riot. [The charges are still pending.] Most commentators took it as a given that the demonstrators could never have decided all on their own to fight back when the police stormed the crowd with clubs and horses. After all, they came armed with swimming goggles and vinegar-soaked bandanas, so clearly they were ready for battle (never mind that this gear was meant as protection against the inevitable tear gas and pepper spray, which even the most peaceful and law-abiding demonstrators have sadly come to expect from the police). Someone must have orchestrated the violence, told them to pick up bricks, held Molotov-cocktail–making workshops. Why would Clarke do this? Apparently, according to press reports, to seek fame and fortune.

In half a dozen newspaper articles, it was pointed out that John Clarke is not homeless himself, that he—gasp!—lives in a rented bungalow in Scarborough. Even more scandalous: there were other people at the protest who weren't homeless, either. What is the assumption? That activists are always self-interested, out to protect their property values, lower their tuition fees, or get themselves raises? In this context, putting one's body on the line for a set of beliefs about how society should function is seen as somehow fraudulent, even sinister. The young and radical are told to shut up and get a job.

I have known several of OCAP's "professional activists" for years. Some of them first became involved in anti-poverty work in their late teens, through Food Not Bombs, a group that believes food is a basic human right and that you should not need a municipal permit to cook some and share it with people who are hungry.

Some of these young activists could, indeed, get lucrative jobs and move out of their cramped, shared apartments if they wanted to. They are staggeringly resourceful and well educated, and some of them are so wily with a Linux operating system that they could easily be one of those teenage dot-com millionaires.

But they have chosen a different route, one that flatly rejects a value system in which the only acceptable use of our skills and talents is to trade them for money and power. Instead, they are using those highly marketable skills to work for power dispersal: to convince the least empowered members of Ontario society that they have powers—to organize collectively, to defend themselves against brutality and abuse, to claim shelter; powers that are going unused.

The Ontario Coalition Against Poverty exists for the sole purpose of empowering the poor and the homeless, which is why it is so very unjust that last week's protest was presented as the scheming handiwork of a single man who uses the poor as props and pawns. The Coalition is one of the very few anti-poverty groups that emphasizes organizing, as opposed to mere charity or advocacy. Within OCAP, poor people are not simply mouths to feed or bodies that need sleeping bags. They are something else entirely: a constituency that has a right to be heard. Finding a way for the homeless to recognize their political rights and take on their opponents is an extraordinarily difficult task, which is why OCAP is frequently held up as a success story by activists around the world.

How do you organize the homeless, the transient, the poor? We know that workers are organized in factories, homeowners in their neighbourhoods, students in their schools. But OCAP's constituency is, by definition, dispersed and constantly on the move. And while workers and students can become political lobbies by forming unions and going on strike, the homeless have already been discarded by every institution they could possibly disrupt.

Obstacles such as these have led most anti-poverty groups to conclude that the poor and the homeless need to be spoken for and acted on. Except for OCAP, which is trying to create a space for the poor to speak, and to act, for themselves. And this is where things gets complicated: most of us don't really want to hear the anger in their voices, see the rage in their actions.

Which is why so many people are pissed off at John Clarke. His crime isn't organizing a riot. It is refusing to clean up poverty for the benefit of cameras and politicians. The Coalition doesn't ask its members to abide by the genteel protocols of polite protest. And it doesn't tell angry people they shouldn't be angry, especially when confronted by some of the very same police officers who beat them in back alleys or the politicians who write laws that cost them their homes.

John Clarke didn't organize a riot and neither did OCAP. They just didn't stop it.

II

FENCING IN DEMOCRACY

II

FENCING IN DEMOCRACY

TRADE AND TRADE-OFFS

[In which citizens discover that the
true price of "free trade" is the
power to govern themselves]

Democracy in Shackles
Who benefits from free trade?

June 2001

During the April 2001 Summit of the Americas in Quebec City, U.S. President George W. Bush proclaimed that the proposed Free Trade Area of the Americas (FTAA) would help usher in "a hemisphere of liberty." Explicitly linking globalization and democracy, Bush argued that "people who operate in open economies eventually demand more open societies."

Does globalization really foster democracy? It depends on the kind of globalization we create. The current system simply outsources decision making to opaque and non-representative institutions, but there are other choices available. At home and on the world stage, democracy is a choice, one that demands constant vigilance and renewal.

President Bush seems to have a different vision. Like so many defenders of the current global economic model, he argues that democracy is not so much an active choice as a trickle-down effect of economic growth: free markets create free peoples. Would that democracy really were such a laissez-faire matter. Unfortunately, investors have proven themselves all too willing to support oppressive monarchies like Saudi Arabia's, or Communist authoritarianism in China, as long as these regimes crack open markets to foreign companies. In the race for cheap labour and precious natural resources, pro-democracy movements are often trampled.

Sure, capitalism thrives in representative democracies that embrace pro-market policies such as privatization and deregulation. But what about when citizens make democratic choices that aren't so popular with foreign investors? What happens when they decide to nationalize the phone company, for instance, or to exert greater control over their oil and mineral wealth? The bodies tell the story.

When Guatemala's democratically elected government introduced sweeping land ownership reforms in the 1950s, breaking up the monopoly held by the U.S.'s United Fruit Company, the country was bombed and the government ousted. At the time, the U.S. claimed it was an inside job, but nine years later, president Dwight D. Eisenhower reflected that, "We had to get rid of a Communist government that had taken over." When General Suharto staged his bloody coup in Indonesia in 1965, he did so with co-operation from the United States and Europe. Roland Challis, the BBC's Southeast Asia correspondent at the time, maintains that "getting British companies and the World Bank back in there was part of the deal." Similarly, it was "free market" forces in the United States that instigated the military overthrow of democratically elected Chilean President Salvador Allende in 1973, eventually leading to his death. (At the time, Henry Kissinger famously commented that a country shouldn't be allowed to "go Communist due to the irresponsibility of its own people.")

The current open talk in Washington about the need to unseat Venezuelan president Hugo Chavez shows that this deadly logic didn't die with the Cold War. But these days, the free market's interference with democracy usually takes subtler forms. It's a directive from the International Monetary Fund requiring governments to introduce user fees in health care, or to slash billions from public services, or to privatize a water system. It's a plan cooked up by the World Bank to erect a massive dam, implemented without consulting the communities displaced by the project, ones whose way of life will disappear. It's a World Bank report calling for more "flexibility" in the labour market of a heavily indebted country—including restrictions on collective bargaining—in order to attract foreign investors. (If they resist and defend themselves, they may well find themselves classified as terrorists, and all means to suppress them will become permissible.)

And sometimes the interference is a complaint to the World Trade Organization that public ownership of a national postal service "discriminates" against a foreign courier company. It's a trade war waged against countries that decide, democratically, to ban hormone-treated beef or to provide free AIDS drugs to their citizens. It's the incessant clamouring for tax cuts from business lobbies in every country, based on the ever-present threat that capital will flee if we don't grant the corporations' up-to-the-minute wish list. Whatever the methods employed, "free markets" rarely stand by and tolerate truly free peoples.

When we talk about the relationship between globalization and democracy, we need to look not only at whether nations have won the right to cast ballots every four or five years but also at whether citizens still consider those ballots meaningful. We must look not only for the presence of electoral democracy but also examine the day-to-day quality and depth of those liberties. Hundreds of thousands take to the streets outside trade meetings not because they oppose trade itself but because the very real need for jobs and investment is systematically being used to undermine all our democracies. The unacceptable trade is the one that erodes sovereign rights in exchange for foreign investment.

What I dislike most about the trickle-down democracy argument is the dishonour it pays to all the people who fought, and fight still, for genuine democratic change in their countries, whether for the right to vote, or to have access to land, or to form unions. Democracy isn't the work of the market's invisible hand; it is the work of real hands. It is often stated, for instance, that the North American Free Trade Agreement is bringing democracy to Mexico. In fact, workers, students, indigenous groups and radical intellectuals are the ones slowly forcing democratic reforms on Mexico's intransigent elite. NAFTA, by widening the gap between rich and poor, makes their struggle more militant, and more difficult.

In the place of such messy, disruptive, real-world democratic movements, President Bush offers a calm, soothing lullaby: just relax and wait for your rights to come to you. But contrary to this lethargic vision of trickle-down democracy, globalization in its current form doesn't bring liberty. Neither does the free market or the ready availability of Big Macs. Real democracy—true decision-making power in the people's hands—is always demanded, never granted.

The Free Trade Area of the Americas
The leaders may agree, but on the streets of Latin American cities, the debate is raging

March 2001

Next Friday, trade ministers from the thirty-four countries negotiating the Free Trade Area of the Americas will meet in Buenos Aires. Many in Latin America predict that the ministers will be greeted with protests much larger than the ones that exploded in Seattle in 1999.

The FTAA's cheerleaders like to pretend that their only critics are white college kids from Harvard and McGill who just don't understand how much "the poor" are "clamouring" for the FTAA. Will this public display of Latin American opposition to the trade deal change all that? Don't be silly.

Mass protests in the developing world don't register in our discussions about trade in the West. No matter how many people take to the streets of Buenos Aires, Mexico City or São Paulo, defenders of corporate-driven globalization just keep on insisting that every possible objection lobbed their way was dreamed up in Seattle by somebody with newly matted dreadlocks slurping a latte.

When we talk about trade, we often focus—and rightly so—on who is getting richer and who is getting poorer. But there is another divide at play: which countries are presented as diverse, complicated political cultures where citizens have a range of divergent views, and which countries seem to speak on the world stage in an ideological monotone.

In North America and Europe, debates are raging about the failures of the current trading system. And yet such diversity of public opinion is rarely attributed to citizens of Third World countries. Instead, they are lumped into one homogenous entity, spoken for by dubiously elected politicians or, better yet, discredited ones such as Mexico's former president Ernesto Zedillo, now calling for an international campaign against "globophobes."

The truth is that no one can speak on behalf of Latin America's five hundred million inhabitants, least of all Zedillo, whose party's defeat was in large part a repudiation of NAFTA's record. All over the Americas, market liberalization is a subject of extreme dispute. The debate is not over whether foreign investment and trade are desirable—Latin America and the Caribbean are already organized into regional trading blocs such as Mercosur. The debate is about democracy: what terms and conditions will poor countries be told they must meet in order to qualify for admission to the global trade club?

Argentina, the host of next week's FTAA meeting, is currently in open revolt over massive cuts to social spending—almost US$8 billion over three years—that have been introduced in order to qualify for an IMF loan package. Last week, three cabinet ministers resigned, unions staged a general strike and university instructors moved their classes to the streets.

Though anger at wrenching austerity measures has focused primarily on the IMF, across the continent it is rapidly expanding to encompass trade deals such as the proposed FTAA. For proof of the dangers, many Latin Americans look to Mexico. The North American Free Trade Agreement came into force on January 1, 1994, and seven years later, three-quarters of the population of Mexico live in poverty, real wages are lower than they were in 1994 and unemployment is rising. So despite the claims that the rest of Latin America wants a NAFTA to call its own, the central labour associations of Brazil, Argentina, Paraguay and Uruguay—representing twenty million workers—have come out against the plan. They are now calling for countrywide referendums on FTAA membership. [As is Brazilian presidential candidate Lula da Silva who, at the time of writing, was pegged to win the October 2002 elections.]

Brazil, meanwhile, has threatened to boycott the Quebec summit altogether, furious at Canada's ban on Brazilian beef. Ottawa cited safety concerns but Brazilians think it had more to do with Canadian resentment over Brazil's subsidized jet manufacturing. The Brazilian government is also wary that the FTAA will contain protections for drug companies that will threaten its visionary public health policy of providing free generic AIDS drugs to anyone who needs them.

Defenders of free trade would have us believe in the facile equation of trade = democracy. The people who will greet our trade ministers on the streets of Buenos Aires next week are posing a more complex and challenging calculation: how much democracy should they be asked to give up in exchange for trade?

IMF Go to Hell
The people of Argentina have tried the IMF approach; now they want a turn to govern the country

March 2002

On the same day that Argentine President Eduardo Duhalde was embroiled in yet another fruitless negotiation with the International Monetary Fund, a group of Buenos Aires residents were going through a negotiation of a different kind. On a sunny Tuesday earlier this month, they were trying to save themselves from eviction. The residents of 335 Ayacucho, including nineteen children, barricaded themselves inside their home, located just blocks away from the national congress, and refused to leave. On the concrete facade of the house, a hand-printed sign said, "IMF Go to Hell."

It may seem strange that an institution as decidedly macro as the IMF would be implicated in an issue as micro as the Ayacucho eviction. But here in a country where half the population has fallen below the poverty line, it's hard to find any sector of society whose fate does not somehow hinge on the decisions made by the international lender.

Librarians, teachers and other public sector workers, who have been getting paid in hastily printed provincial currencies, won't get paid at all if the provinces agree to stop printing the money, as the IMF is demanding. And if deeper cuts are made to the public sector, as the lender is also insisting, unemployed workers, 30 percent of the workforce, will be even closer to the homelessness and hunger that has led thousands to storm supermarkets demanding food.

And if a solution isn't found to the recently declared medical state of emergency, it will certainly affect a woman I met on the outskirts of Buenos Aires. In a fit of shame and desperation, she pulled up her blouse and showed me the open wound and hanging tubes from a stomach operation that her doctor was not able to stitch up or dress due to a chronic shortage of medical supplies.

Maybe it seems rude to talk about such matters here. Economic analysis is supposed to be about the peg to the dollar, "pesoification," and the dangers of "stagflation"—not children losing homes or elderly women's gaping wounds. Yet the reckless advice being hurled at Argentina's government from beyond its borders perhaps demands a little personalizing.

In free-market circles, the consensus is that the IMF should see Argentina's crisis not as an obstacle to further austerity but as an opportunity: the country is so desperate for cash, the reasoning goes, that it will do whatever the IMF wants. "During a crisis is when you need to act, it's when Congress is most receptive," explains Winston Fritsch, chairman of Dresdner Bank AG's Brazilian unit.

The most draconian suggestion has come from Ricardo Cabellero and Rudiger Dornbusch, a pair of MIT economists writing in *The Financial Times*. "It's time to get radical," they say. Argentina "must temporarily surrender its sovereignty on all financial issues . . . give up much of its monetary, fiscal, regulatory and asset management sovereignty for an extended period, say five years." The country's economy—its "spending, money printing and tax administration"—should be controlled by "foreign agents," including "a board of experienced foreign central bankers."

In a nation still scarred by the disappearance of thirty thousand people during the 1976 to 1983 military dictatorship, only a "foreign agent" would have the nerve to say, as the MIT team does, that "somebody has to run the country with a tight grip." Yet it seems that repression is the necessary pre-condition to the real work of saving the country, which, according to Cabellero and Dornbusch, involves prying open markets, introducing deeper spending cuts and, of course, a "massive privatization campaign."

It's the usual recipe, only this time, there's a hitch: Argentina has already done it all. As the IMF's model student throughout the nineties, it flung open its economy (which is why it's been so easy for capital to flee since the crisis began). As far as Argentina's supposedly wild public spending goes, a full third goes directly to servicing the external debt. Another third goes to pension funds, which have already been privatized. The remaining third—some of which actually goes to health care, education and social assistance—has fallen far behind population growth, which is why shipments of donated food and medicine are arriving by boat from Spain.

As for "massive privatization," Argentina has dutifully sold off so many of its services, from trains to phones, that the only examples of further assets Cabellero and Dornbusch can think of privatizing are the country's ports and customs offices.

No wonder so many who sang Argentina's praises in the past are now rushing to blame its economic collapse exclusively on national greed and corruption. "If a country thinks they're going to get aid from the United States, and they're stealing money, they're just not going to get it," George W. Bush said in Mexico last week. Argentina "is going to have to make some tough calls."

Argentina's population, which has been in open revolt against its political, financial and legal elite for months, hardly has to be lectured on the need for good governance. In the last federal election, more people spoiled their ballots than voted for any single politician. The most popular write-in candidate was a cartoon character named Clemente, chosen because he has no hands and therefore cannot steal.

But it's hard to believe that the IMF is going to be the one to clean up Argentina's culture of payola and impunity, especially since one of the conditions the lender has placed on new funds is that Argentina's courts stop prosecuting bankers who illegally pulled their money out of the country, drastically deepening the crisis. And as long as the destruction of this country is presented as a uniquely national pathology, it will conveniently keep the spotlight off the IMF itself.

In the familiar narrative of an impoverished country begging the world for a "bailout," a crucial development is being obscured: many people here have little interest in the IMF's money, especially when it will clearly cost them so much. Instead, they are busily building new political counter-powers to both their own failed political structures and the IMF.

Tens of thousands of residents have organized themselves into neighbourhood assemblies, networked at the city and national levels. In town squares, parks and on street corners, neighbours discuss ways of making their democracies more accountable and filling in where government has failed. They are talking about creating a "citizens' congress" to demand transparency and accountability from politicians. They are discussing participatory budgets and shorter political terms, while organizing communal kitchens for the unemployed. The president, who wasn't even elected, is scared enough of this growing political force that he has begun calling the "*asambleas*" antidemocratic.

There is reason to pay attention. The *asambleas* are also talking about how to kick-start local industries and renationalize assets. And they could go even further. Argentina, as the obedient pupil for decades, miserably failed by its IMF professors, shouldn't be begging for loans; it should be demanding reparations.

The IMF had its chance to run Argentina. Now it's the people's turn.

No Place for Local Democracy
When a town gets in the way of a lucrative trade deal, a corporation sues in international court

February 2001

Anyone still unclear about why the police are constructing a modern-day Bastille around Quebec City in preparation for the unveiling of the Free Trade Area of the Americas should take a look at a case being heard by the British Columbia Supreme Court. In 1991, Metalclad, a U.S. waste management company, bought a closed-down toxic treatment facility in Guadalcazar, Mexico. The company wanted to build a huge hazardous-waste dump and promised to clean up the mess left behind by the previous owners. But in the years that followed, they expanded operations without seeking local approval, earning little goodwill in Guadalcazar.

Residents lost trust that Metalclad was serious about cleaning up, feared continued groundwater contamination and eventually decided that the foreign company was not welcome. In 1995, when the landfill was ready to open, the town and state intervened with what legislative powers they had available: the city denied Metalclad a building permit, and the state declared that the area around the site was part of an ecological reserve.

By this point, the North American Free Trade Agreement—

including its controversial "Chapter 11" clause, which allows investors to sue governments—was in full effect. So Metalclad launched a Chapter 11 challenge, claiming Mexico was "expropriating" its investment. The complaint was heard last August in Washington, D.C., by a three-person arbitration panel. Metalclad asked for US$90 million, and was awarded $16.7 million. Using a rare third-party appeal mechanism, Mexico chose to challenge the ruling before the British Columbia Supreme Court.

The Metalclad case is a vivid illustration of what critics mean when they charge that free trade deals amount to a "bill of rights for multinational corporations." Metalclad has successfully played the victim, oppressed by what NAFTA calls "intervention" and what used to be called "democracy."

As the Metalclad case shows, sometimes democracy breaks out when you least expect it. Maybe it's in a sleepy town or a complacent city, where residents suddenly decide that their politicians haven't done their jobs and it's time for citizens to step in. Community groups form, council meetings are stormed. And sometimes there is a victory: a hazardous mine never gets built, a plan to privatize the local water system is scuttled, a garbage dump is blocked.

Frequently, this community action happens late in the game and earlier decisions are reversed. These outbreaks of grassroots intervention are messy, inconvenient and difficult to predict—but democracy, despite the best-laid plans, sometimes bursts out of council meetings and closed-door committees.

It is precisely this kind of democracy that the Metalclad

panel deemed "arbitrary," and it is why we should all pay attention. Under so-called free trade, governments are losing their ability to be responsive to constituents, to learn from mistakes and to correct them before it's too late. Metalclad's position is that the Mexican government should simply have ignored the local objections. And there's no doubt that from an investor perspective, it's always easier to negotiate with one level of government than with three.

The catch is that our democracies don't work that way: issues such as waste disposal cut across levels of government, affecting not just trade but drinking water, health, ecology and tourism. Furthermore, it is in local communities that the real impacts of free trade policies are felt most acutely.

Cities are asked to absorb the people pushed off their land by industrial agriculture, or forced to leave their provinces due to cuts in federal employment programs. Cities and towns have to find shelter for those made homeless by deregulated rental markets, and municipalities have to deal with the mess of failed privatization experiments—all with an eroded tax base. The trade deals may be negotiated internationally, but it's the locals who have to drink the water.

There is a move among many municipal politicians to demand increased powers in response to this off-loading. For instance, citing the Washington Metalclad ruling, Vancouver City Council passed a resolution last month petitioning "the federal government to refuse to sign any new trade and investment agreements, such as . . . the Free Trade Area of the Americas, that include investor-state provisions similar to the ones included in NAFTA." And on Monday, the mayors of Canada's largest cities launched a campaign for greater constitutional powers. "[Cities] are listed in the constitution of the late 1800s between saloons and asylums and that's where we get our power, so we can be offloaded [and] downloaded," explained Joanne Monaghan, president of the Federation of Canadian Municipalities.

Cities and towns need decision-making powers commensurate with their increased responsibilities, or they will simply be turned into passive dumping grounds for the toxic fallout of free trade. Sometimes, as in Guadalcazar, the dumping is plain to see.

Most of the time it is better hidden.

[*In May 2001, the British Columbia Supreme Court upheld the NAFTA tribunal's findings, and Mexico paid Metalclad more than US$16 million in October 2001.*]

The War on Unions
In Mexico, factory workers demand that Nike honour its word

January 2001

Marion Traub-Werner was in Toronto visiting her family when the call came: eight hundred garment workers had walked off the job at a factory in Mexico. She caught the next plane to Mexico City and was meeting with workers within hours.

For Traub-Werner, this wasn't just any strike. "It was the one we've been waiting for," she says. This factory was producing sweatshirts that bear the insignias of the universities of Michigan, Oregon, Arizona, Indiana and North Carolina. The factory's biggest client is Nike, which has sports apparel contracts with these schools and many others.

For the past five years, Marion Traub-Werner has been one of the key organizers of the growing anti-sweatshop student movement in North America, helping to found United Students Against Sweatshops, now active on 175 campuses. The students have been locked in a bitter dispute with the companies that produce clothing for their schools, and their most public battles have been with sporting goods giant Nike.

At issue is who should be trusted to regulate and monitor the factories in the US$2.5 billion college apparel market.

Nike has consistently claimed it can solve the problem itself: it says it has a strong code of conduct and is part of the Fair Labor Association, set up by former U.S. president Bill Clinton. It also hires outside accounting firms to make sure the seven hundred factories that produce its goods are playing by the rules. [*The argument that accounting firms have an impartial relationship with the corporations they are paid to audit has become markedly less popular since the Enron/Andersen debacle.*]

The students have rejected this route, saying that corporations cannot be expected to monitor themselves. They have instead pressured their schools and universities to join the Workers' Rights Consortium, a group that advocates truly independent monitoring, free of company control.

To outsiders, it has seemed an arcane battle between competing acronyms: the FLA *v.* the WRC. But at the Kuk-Dong garment factory in Atlixco, Mexico, the dispute has just taken on a human face. Kuk-Dong was one of Nike's test factories, visited by Nike-hired monitors on several occasions.

Today, the students will go public with a damning videotaped interview with a Kuk-Dong worker, footage they say shows that Nike's code of conduct is being violated. On the video, which I viewed yesterday, a young Mexican woman speaks of poverty wages, hunger, of getting sick on the job and not being allowed time off. When asked how old she is, she replies, "Fifteen."

According to Nike's code of conduct, the company will not employ garment workers younger than sixteen. Nike says she may have falsified documents to land the job.

Document fraud is, in fact, widespread in Mexico, but underage workers often claim that they were coached to lie by the local companies' own recruiters.

There are other factors in the Kuk-Dong case that call Nike's monitoring methods into question. Nike claims that the workers who produce its goods have the right to freedom of association, and when I spoke yesterday to Vada Manager, Nike's director of Global Issues Management, he insisted, "We are not anti-union."

But workers say that when they decided to throw out the "company union" that failed to represent their interests, five of their most outspoken representatives were fired. (So-called company unions, in bed with management, are commonplace in Mexico, where independent unions are treated as a barrier to foreign investment.)

Last Tuesday, the workers went on strike to protest the firing of their leaders: eight hundred people walked away from their sewing machines and occupied their factory. According to Josephina Hernandez, one of the fired organizers, "What we are asking for is an end to the corrupt union and for an independent union formed by workers."

The results, once again, were disastrous. On Thursday, riot police, led by the leader of the company union, swept in and put an end to the protest, beating workers and sending fifteen to hospital. The attacks were so brutal that roughly two hundred workers have decided not to return to work at the factory, even though the strike is over, fearing management retribution. Freedom of association, a right according to Mexican law and Nike's own code of conduct, is clearly not a reality at the Kuk-Dong factory.

Vada Manager says the last order Nike placed with Kuk-Dong—for fleece sweatshirts—was filled in December. He says Nike will decide whether to place further orders based on the recommendations of its "mediator on the scene."

The factory workers and university students, working together in Mexico, want something else. They don't want Nike to flee an ugly scene to save face but to stay and prove that its code of conduct is more than empty words. "We want Nike to put pressure on Kuk-Dong to negotiate directly with the workers," says Traub-Werner. "It's a long-term approach, but we think a more lasting one."

[*The Kuk-Dong workers went on a hunger strike, and Nike eventually pressured the factory to allow the strik-ing workers to return to their jobs. In September 2001 the workers won the right to form an independent union, which, according to the U.S. human rights group Global Exchange, "is a precedent-setting victory" that could lead to further worker organization and independent unions in Mexico's factories.*]

The NAFTA Track Record
After seven years, the numbers extolling the virtues of the agreement just don't add up

April 2001

This piece was a response to an article written in The Globe and Mail *by Canada's former prime minister Brian Mulroney, the man who negotiated both the Free Trade Agreement between Canada and the U.S. and the North American Free Trade Agreement, which brought Mexico into the deal. In the article, he argued in favour of a further expansion of NAFTA, to include the entire hemisphere (the proposed Free Trade Area of the Americas). Mulroney's position hinges on his belief that NAFTA has been an unqualified success for all three countries. At the time the debate was published, Quebec City was preparing to host the Summit of the Americas, the meeting of thirty-four heads of state to launch the FTAA. Activists from across the Americas were planning huge counter-demonstrations.*

Brian Mulroney thinks the numbers are his friends. He proudly points to the percentage of Canada's gross domestic product now made up by exports to the United States—40 percent! The number of jobs created by trade—four in five! And Mexico's status as an important U.S. trading partner—second only to Canada! These numbers are a vindication, our former prime minister believes, for the free trade deals he negotiated first with the United States, then with Mexico.

He still doesn't get it: those numbers aren't his friends; they're his worst enemy. Opposition to free trade has grown, and grown more vocal, precisely because private wealth has soared without translating into anything that can be clearly identified as the public good. It's not that critics don't know how much money is being made under free trade—it's that we know all too well.

While there's no shortage of numbers pointing to increases in exports and investment, the trickle-down effects promised as the political incentive for deregulation—a cleaner environment, higher wages, better working conditions, less poverty—have either been pitifully incremental or non-existent.

The labour and environmental side agreements tacked on the North American Free Trade Agreement have a spectacularly poor track record. Today, 75 percent of Mexico's population lives in poverty, up from 49 percent in 1981.

Trade may be creating jobs in Canada but not enough of them to keep up with the number of jobs that have been eliminated—by 1997, there had been a net loss of 276,000 jobs, according to the Canadian Centre for Policy Alternatives.

Total pollution from manufacturing has doubled in Mexico since NAFTA was introduced, according to a Tufts University study. And the United States has become a climate-change renegade, chucking out its Kyoto commitments wholesale. It turns out that defiant unilateralism is the ultimate luxury item in the free trade era, reserved for the ultra rich.

There is always a ready excuse for why the wealth liberated by free trade is stuck at the top: a recession, the deficit, the peso crisis, political corruption and now another looming recession. There is always a reason why it should be spent on another tax break instead of social or environmental programs.

What Mulroney doesn't understand is that only economists worship wealth creation as an abstraction, only the very rich fetishize it as an end in itself. The rest of us are interested in those rising numbers on the trade ledger for what they can buy: does increased trade and investment mean we can afford to rebuild our health care system? Can we keep our promises to end child poverty? Can we fund better schools? Build affordable housing? Can we afford to invest in cleaner energy sources? Do we work less, have more leisure time? In short, do we have a better, more just, sustainable society?

The opposite is the case.

As Mulroney was kind enough to admit, "Free trade is part of a whole that includes the GST [Canada's Goods and Services Tax], deregulation, privatization, and a concerted effort to reduce deficits, inflation, and interest rates." These are the domestic preconditions of playing the global trade game—a package that, taken together, guarantees that the numbers Mulroney touts so proudly do little to address stagnant wages, economic disparities and a deepening environmental crisis.

And when economic growth is severed from meaningful

measures of social progress, thinking people begin to lose faith in the system. They start to ask difficult questions not only about trade but also about how economists measure progress and value. Why can't we measure ecological deficits, as well as economic growth? What is the real social cost—in cuts to education, in increased homelessness—of the whole package of policies referred to by Mulroney?

These are the types of questions that will be heard in Quebec City this week. They will come from people such as José Bové, the French dairy farmer whose campaign is not against McDonald's but against an agricultural model that sees food purely as an industrial commodity rather than the centrepiece of national culture and family life. They will come from health care workers questioning a trade system that defends patents for AIDS drugs more vigorously than millions of human lives. They will come from university students, paying more for their "public" education every year, while their schools have been invaded by ads and their research departments are being privatized one commercially sponsored study at a time.

The slogan People before Profits is dismissed as unfocused by free trade defenders, but it neatly encapsulates the sentiment running through the campaigns that are converging in Quebec City. The argument for barrelling ahead with the Free Trade Area of the Americas is based on an unshakable ideological belief that what's good for business will be good for everyone—eventually. Even if that dubious argument is true, the timeline is unacceptable. According to the governor of the Bank of Mexico, at the current rate of economic growth, it will be sixty years before Mexico doubles its per capita income and ends its extreme poverty.

What the protesters are saying is that human dignity and environmental sustainability are too important to be patiently prayed for like rain during a drought. They should not be belated side effects but the very foundations of our economic policies.

Thankfully, the protesters are resisting the pressure to come up with a one-size-fits-all alternative to free trade and are, instead, defending the right to genuine global diversity and self-determination. Rather than one solution, there are thousands, slowly coalescing into an alternative economic model. In Cochabamba, Bolivia, that means insisting that water is not a commodity but a human right, even if it means throwing out the international water conglomerate Bechtel. In British Columbia, it means First Nations and non-native rural communities demanding the right to manage "community forests," which combine selective logging, tourism and local industry, as opposed to granting industrial tree-farm licences to logging multinationals. In Mexico and Guatemala, it means coffee farm co-operatives that guarantee a living wage and ecological diversity.

Some defenders of free trade say that if the protesters in Quebec City were serious, they would be on the other side of the chain-link fence that has been built to protect the delegates and that now physically divides the city. They say that protesters should be politely negotiating side agreements on labour, democracy and environmental standards.

But thirteen years after the first free trade agreement

with the United States, it's not the details of the FTAA agreement (we still don't know them) but the economic model itself that is under fire—the numbers just don't add up.

Displaying his usual diplomacy, Prime Minister Jean Chrétien last week told the newspaper *Le Devoir* that thousands are coming to Quebec City to "protest and blah blah blah." Quite the opposite. They're coming to Quebec to protest because they've had it with the "blah blah blah."

POST–SEPTEMBER 11 POSTSCRIPT

The following article was written eight months after the Quebec summit. It is included here because after the attacks in New York and Washington, D.C., the trade-offs for increased trade became even more stark.

In the name of fighting terrorism, the United States is demanding that Canada dramatically toughen security at its borders, as well as give up a great deal of control over them to U.S. security officers. Canada could scarcely be in a worse bargaining position: thanks to free trade, 87 percent of our exports go to the U.S. and almost half of our economy is now directly dependent on an open border.

Many Canadians see some border integration as the unavoidable price of protecting the $700 billion annual trade relationship with the United States. But Canadians are being asked to give up more than border control. We are also being asked to hand over a chunk of the economic dividends of years of economic austerity. Finance Minister Paul Martin's "security budget," delivered on December 10, throws $1.2 billion directly at the border. Some of it is designed to protect Canadians from terrorists, but much of it must be seen for what it is: a new public subsidy for multinational corporations.

When Canadians accepted cutbacks to health care, unemployment insurance and other social programs, we were told that this austerity was necessary to attract foreign investors. We weren't trading our social programs for free trade, the boosters said—on the contrary, only free trade would generate the kind of prosperity needed to rebuild our social programs.

But there's a hitch. Just as Canadians were starting to imagine spending some of our recent national prosperity on new programs, it turns out that the budget surplus will not be used to make people more secure. It will be used to make trade more secure, to "keep our borders open," as Martin said.

The proceeds of cross-border trade are going back into the border itself: to make it a terrorist-fighting and free-trade-flowing superborder. We are going to have "the most modern border in the world," Martin enthused. This, it turns out, is the legacy of all the years of belt tightening: not a better society but a really great border.

The plan is to create multi-tier border crossings that are at once open for business but closed to "unwanted" people. This is no easy task, since migration of people and trade in goods tend to be interrelated.

That's why Martin's plan to open and close the border at once is so costly: $395 million to screen refugees and immigrants, $58 million to make border crossing smoother for frequent business travellers, $500 million to crack down on illegal immigrants, $600 million over six years to improve the traffic flow.

Let's pause for the irony. Free trade was supposed to lower the costs of moving goods across borders, thereby encouraging new investment. Now we have become so dependent on trade (and the U.S. has become so mistrustful of our ability to police ourselves) that we are spending hundreds of millions of new dollars just to keep the trade flowing.

Put another way, costs that used to be absorbed by the private sector in the form of export and import duties and tariffs have been transferred to taxpayers in the form of security costs. The border, the promise of so much prosperity, is turning into an economic sinkhole.

Annette Verschuren, president of Home Depot Canada, applauded Monday's budget, saying, "We depend on the border to ensure that our goods get to our stores, and anything that speeds it up reduces our costs."

Are the new security costs an unavoidable price to pay for our economic stability? Perhaps. But they should at least send a cautionary message to our politicians who are pushing to expand the North American Free Trade Agreement into the entire hemisphere.

Free trade has already taken a severe toll on our social programs and our ability to make sovereign immigration and refugee policy. It is now costing us billions in security dollars. Can we at least stop calling it "free"?

Higher Fences at the Border
Migrant workers know that as barriers to trade come down, barriers to people go up

November 2000

When the right-wing Canadian Alliance candidate Betty Granger used the phrase "Asian invasion" last week, it was a flashback to Second World War "yellow peril" rhetoric and she was forced to resign. But there was another pearl of wisdom the candidate shared in the same speech, one that went largely unnoticed. Referring to boats of Chinese immigrants seized off the British Columbia coast, she said, "There was a realization that what was coming off these boats was not the best clientele you would want for this country."

Clientele. It doesn't have the same xenophobic ring as "Asian invasion"; in fact, it sounds positively clinical. But it may be more dangerous, especially because it is an idea that is not relegated to the fringe of the Alliance party but lies at the very centre of the immigration debate.

In rich countries like Canada, we often talk about migrant labourers as "clients," while our country, with its public health care and reasonably healthy job market, is the product these clients would like to purchase. Since there are millions of migrants shopping around, we can carefully assess, as Granger did, whether they are "the best" clients available.

"Betty Granger just expressed out there in the open a prevailing, but false, idea about immigrants, which is that immigrants are people who come to be served," says Fely Villasïn, co-ordinator of the advocacy group Intercede for the Rights of Domestic Workers, Caregivers and Newcomers.

The truth is that mass migration is not a form of homeland shopping: it is the flip side of the free trade policies our government so actively pursues. People don't mortgage their futures to get on rusty boats because they are in the market for something a little more upscale. They do it because changes at home have left them without a job, without land, without choices.

It could have been a war or a hurricane. But it could also have been less dramatic shifts: farmland converted to export factories or industrial plantations, or drowned out by megadams. Last week, Nelson Mandela presented a report assessing the global impact of megadams, projects traditionally seen by the World Bank as necessary preconditions to joining the global economy. The report, published by the World Commission on Dams, found that the projects were dramatically increasing migration flows—1.2 million people will be displaced by China's Three Gorges Dam alone.

Residents forced off their land by dams and other development schemes move to cities, and they also board boats destined for other countries. When Canada lobbies for more investment opportunities for our energy companies, all Canadians become complicit in this mass displacement of people—displaced by neo-liberal globalization itself.

But migrant workers, who now number 70 million to 85

million globally, are more than the unseen side effect of "free trade." Once displaced, they also enter the free market, not as clients but as commodities, selling the only thing they have left: their labour.

Our government, we are told, favours a level playing field in the international trade of commodities. We have championed the World Trade Organization, and we are leading the charge to expand the North American Free Trade Agreement into Central and South America. We fight for the principle of treating foreign companies as we do our own: no unfair domestic subsidies, no extra regulations, no strings attached to investment.

But when the commodity being traded across borders is labour, these protections and principles disappear. Every year, roughly 200,000 migrant workers come to Canada to work as low-wage cleaners, seamstresses, nannies and seasonal farm workers. And yet our government has flatly refused to ratify the International Convention on the Protection of the Rights of All Migrant Workers and Members of Their Families, an agreement that would protect them from discrimination.

Instead, we have the Live-In Caregiver Program, which legislates unequal treatment for housekeepers and nannies who come to Canada and live in their employers' homes. Under the program, migrants must work full-time without landed immigrant status or basic labour protections for twenty-four months over a three-year period. Only if they meet the work quota can they can apply for residency. If they don't, they are deported.

Because they live in their workplace, unpaid overtime is rampant and sexual abuse is common. But because their immigration status depends on keeping these jobs, most workers are not inclined to complain.

In an Orwellian twist, corporations have seamlessly adopted the language of human rights: Wal-Mart and Exxon, trading cargo across borders, demand "fair and equal treatment" and "non-discrimination clauses." Meanwhile, humans are increasingly treated like cargo, with no rights at all.

Betty Granger said the migrants who come to Canada are "not the best clientele." In fact, it is Canadians who are the clientele for cheap migrant labour: we purchase it for our homes, farms, restaurants and factories. Only when we recognize that we are already participating in this free trade in people—and not generously opening our borders to the world's needy—will migrants receive the protection that is their human right.

Making–and Breaking–the Rules
Mr. Prime Minister, we are not anti-globalization, we are the true internationalists

October 2001

In September 2001, the European Union President and Belgian Prime Minister Guy Verhofstadt wrote an open letter to the "anti-globalization" movement. "Your concerns as anti-globalists are extremely valid," he said in the letter, "but to find the right solutions to these valid questions we need more globalization, not less. That is the paradox of anti-globalization. Globalization can, after all, serve the cause of good just as much as it can serve the cause of evil. What we need is a global ethical approach to the environment, labour relations and monetary policy. In other words, the challenge that we are faced with today is not how to thwart globalization but instead how to give it an ethical foundation." (To read the prime minister's letter in full, see www.premier.fgov.be/topics/press/e_press23.html.

After the letter sparked considerable controversy, Verhofstadt convened the "International Conference on Globalization" in Ghent, Belgium, and invited a series of speakers, including Naomi Klein, to respond to his letter. This is the speech (slightly expanded) delivered at the event.

Prime Minister Verhofstadt,

Thank you for your letter to "the anti-globalization protesters."
It is extremely significant that you have initiated such a public debate. I must admit that I have, over the past few years,
gotten used to something else from world leaders: either
being dismissed as part of a marginal travelling circus, or
invited into closed-door negotiations that lack any
accountability.

I had begun to think that marginalization and co-optation
were the only two choices available to globalization critics.
Oh, and criminalization. Make that three choices. Genuine
debates on these issues—the open airing of different world
views—are extremely rare amid the tear gas and posturing.

But perhaps there aren't as many anti-globalization
protesters here today as you would have liked, Mr. Prime
Minister. I think that's partly because many in the movement don't see us here as their representatives. Many are
tired of being spoken for and about. They are demanding a
more direct form of political participation.

There is also much debate about what this movement
stands for. For instance, I strongly object to your term "anti-
globalization." The way I see it, I am part of a network of
movements that is fighting not against globalization but for
deeper and more responsive democracies, locally, nationally
and internationally. This network is as global as capitalism
itself. And no, that's not a "paradox," as you claim.

It's time to stop conflating basic principles of internationalism and interconnectedness—principles only Luddites
and narrow nationalists oppose—with a specific economic

model that is very much in dispute. At issue is not the merits of internationalism. All the activists I know are fierce internationalists. Rather, we are challenging the internationalization of a single economic model: neo-liberalism.

If we are to have genuine debates like this one, what we are calling "globalization" must be recast not just as an inevitable stage in human evolution but as a profoundly political process: a set of deliberate, debatable and reversible choices about how to globalize.

Part of the confusion about what we mean when we use the term "globalization" stems from the fact that this particular economic model has a tendency to treat trade not as one part of internationalism but the overarching infrastructure of it. It gradually swallows everything else—culture, human rights, the environment, democracy itself—inside the perimeters of trade.

When we debate this model, we are not discussing the merits of trading goods and services across borders but the effects of profound corporatization around the world; the ways in which "the commons" is being transformed and rearranged—cut back, privatized, deregulated—all in the name of participating and competing in the global trading system. What is being designed at the WTO is not rules for trade but a template for one-size-fits-all government, a kind of "McRule." And it's this template that is under dispute.

Post September 11, Americans are getting an up-close look at these trade-offs as their hospitals, post offices, airports and water systems struggle to deal with a terrorist threat that preys on holes in the public sector. And as millions lose their jobs, many more are learning that the social safety net is no longer there to catch them—another trade-off made in the name of trade. In Canada, we are currently making the ultimate trade-off: control over our borders in exchange for continued free trade with the U.S.

Hundreds of thousands are taking to the streets outside trade meetings not because they are against trade itself but because the real need for trade and investment is systematically being used to erode the very principles of self-government. "Govern our way or be left out completely" seems to be what passes for multilateralism in the neo-liberal age.

As we discover the vulnerabilities of this economic model, are we able to learn from our mistakes, to measure this model against its own stated objectives and ask if the trade-offs have been worth it? It seems not. The response from politicians since September 11 has been more of the same: tax breaks for businesses and further privatized services, in the U.S. and around the world.

One of the top items on the agenda at next month's [November 2001] World Trade Organization meeting is the General Agreement of Trade in Services, the side agreement that steadily pushes for more market access to public services, including health care, education and water. It also restricts the ability of governments to set and enforce health and environmental standards.

But countries need trade, you say, particularly poor countries, and to have trade there must be rules. Of course. But why not build an international architecture founded on principles of transparency, accountability and self-determination, one that frees people instead of liberating capital?

That would mean enforcing those basic human rights that make self-determination possible, like the right to form independent trade unions, through the International Labour Organization (ILO). It would mean eliminating the policies that systematically keep democracies in shackles: debt, structural adjustment programs, enforced privatization. It would also mean making good on long-delayed promises of land reform and reparations for slavery. International rules could be designed to make genuine democracy and empowerment more than empty phrases.

No doubt you agree with this sentiment, Mr. Prime Minister. In fact, reading your letter, I was struck by the similarity of our stated goals. You call for "a global ethical approach to the environment, labour relations and monetary policy." I want those things too. So the real question is why are we here, then—what's to debate?

Sadly, what's to debate and what must be debated, or there will never be peace outside the summits, is the track record. Not words but deeds. Not good intentions—there's never any shortage of these—but the grim and worsening facts: wage stagnation, dramatic increases in the disparity between rich and poor and the erosion of basic services around the world.

Despite the rhetoric of openness and freedom, we see new and higher fences constantly going up: around refugee centres in the Australian desert, around two million U.S. citizens in prisons, fences turning entire continents like North America and Europe into fortresses, while Africa is locked out. And, of course, the fences that are erected every time world leaders get together to have a meeting.

Globalization was supposed to be about global openness and integration, and yet our societies are steadily becoming more closed, more guarded, requiring ever more security and military might just to maintain the inequitable status quo.

Globalization was also supposed to be about a new system of equality among nations. We were coming together and agreeing to live by the same rules, or so it was said. But it is more evident than ever that the big players are still making the rules and enforcing them, often enforcing them on everyone but themselves—whether it's agricultural and steel subsidies or import tariffs.

These inequalities and asymmetries, always bubbling under the surface, are now impossible to avoid. Many countries that have been through, or are going through, economic crisis— Russia, Thailand, Indonesia and Argentina, to name just a few—would have appreciated the extreme government intervention just launched to save the U.S. economy, instead of the austerity prescribed by the IMF. The governor of Virginia explained the U.S.'s tax cuts and subsidy measures by saying that America's recession "is not a routine economic downturn." But what makes an economic downturn extraordinary, in need of lavish economic stimulus, versus "routine," in need of austerity and bitter medicine?

The most striking of these recent defiant displays of double standards relates to drug patents. According to World Trade Organization rules, countries are free to break drug patents on life-saving drugs when there is a national emergency. And yet when South Africa tried to do it for AIDS drugs, it faced a lawsuit from the major drug companies. When Brazil tried to do likewise, it was hauled in front of WTO tribunals. Millions living with AIDS have essentially been told that their lives count less than drug patents, less than debt repayment, that there is simply no money to save them. The World Bank says it's time to focus on prevention, not cures, which is tantamount to a death sentence for millions.

And yet earlier this month, Canada decided to override Bayer's patent for Cipro, the favoured antibiotic to treat anthrax. We ordered a million tablets of a generic version. "These are extraordinary and unusual times," a spokeswoman for Health Canada said. "Canadians expect and demand that their government will take all steps necessary to protect their health and safety." It should be noted that Canada still hasn't had a single diagnosed case of anthrax.

Although the decision was later reversed after Bayer lowered its prices, the same logic was at work: when it comes to rich countries, rules are for other people. Vulnerability to abstract economic theory has become the great class divider. The rich and powerful countries seem to be able to pick and choose when to follow the rules, but poor nations are told that economic orthodoxies must govern their every move, that they must throw themselves at the mercy of a free market ideology that even its architects disregard when it's not convenient. Poor countries that put the needs of their citizens before the demands of foreign investors are vilified as protectionists, even communists. And yet the protectionist policies that fuelled Britain's industrial revolution were so rampant, that it was illegal to bury a corpse without first proving that the funeral shroud had been woven in a British mill.

What does this have to do with our debate? Too often, we pretend inequalities persist and deepen only because of national idiosyncrasies, or because we haven't happened on the right set of rules, the perfect formula, as if these inequalities were little more than some cosmic oversight, or an irregularity in an otherwise functioning system. Always missing from this discussion is the issue of power. So many of the debates that we have about globalization theory are actually about power: who holds it, who is exercising it and who is disguising it, pretending it no longer matters.

But it's no longer enough to say that justice and equality are around the corner and not offer anything but good intentions for collateral. We have just been through a period of tremendous economic prosperity, a time of expansiveness and plenty when core contradictions in this economic model should have been addressed. Now we are entering into a period of contraction, and greater sacrifices are being asked of those who have already sacrificed far too much.

Are we really supposed to be placated by the promise that our problems will be solved with more trade? Tougher protections on drug patents and more privatization? Today's globalizers are like doctors with access to a single drug: whatever the ailment—poverty, migration, climate change, dictatorships, terrorism—the remedy is always more trade.

Mr. Prime Minister, we are not anti-globalization. In fact, we have been going through our own globalization process. And it is precisely because of globalization that the system is in crisis. We know too much. There is too much communication and mobility at the grassroots for the gap to hold. Not just the gap between rich and poor but also between rhetoric and reality. Between what is said and what is done. Between the promise of globalization and its real effects. It's time to close the gap.

THE MARKET SWALLOWS
THE COMMONS

In which access to safe food, clean water
and affordable housing is fenced off—
and anti-capitalism becomes the
hot, new marketing pitch

Genetically Altered Rice
You can't eat public relations

August 2000

"This rice could save a million kids a year." That was the arresting headline on the cover of last week's *Time* magazine. It referred to golden rice, a newly market-ready variety of genetically engineered grain that contains extra beta carotene, which helps the body produce vitamin A. All over Asia, millions of malnourished children suffer from vitamin A deficiency, which can lead to blindness and death.

To get their supposed miracle cure off the ground, AstraZeneca, the company that owns marketing rights for golden rice, has offered to donate the grains to poor farmers in countries such as India, where genetically engineered crops have so far met fierce resistance.

It's possible that golden rice could improve the health of millions of children. The problem is that there is no way to separate that powerful emotional claim (and the limited science attached to it) from the overheated political context in which the promise is being made.

GE foods, originally greeted with rubber stamps from governments and indifference from the public, have rapidly become an international repository for anxiety about everything from food safety to corporate-financed science to privatized culture. Opponents argue that the current testing standards fail to take into account the complex web of interrelations that exists among living things. Altered soybeans, for example, may appear safe in a controlled test environment, but how, once grown in nature, will they affect the weeds around them, the insects that feed on them and the crops that cross-pollinate with them?

What has blindsided the agribusiness companies is that the fight has been a battle of the brands as much as one of warring scientific studies. Early on, activists decided to aim their criticism not at agribusiness itself but at the brand-name supermarkets and packaged-food companies that sold products containing "Frankenfoods."

Their brand images tarnished, British supermarkets began pulling products off their shelves, and companies such as Gerber and Frito-Lay went GE-free. In the United States and Canada, environmentalists have set their sights on Kellogg's and Campbell's Soup, parodying their carefully nurtured logos and costly ad campaigns.

At first, the agribusiness companies couldn't figure out how to respond. Even if they could claim that their altered foods had no harmful effects, they couldn't point to direct nutritional benefits either. So that raised the question, Why take a risk? Which is where golden rice comes in. AstraZeneca now has a benefit to point to—not to mention a powerful brand of its own to fight the brand wars with.

Golden rice has all the feel-good ingredients of a strong brand. First, it's golden, as in golden retrievers and gold cards and golden sunsets. Second, unlike other genetically engineered foods, it isn't spliced with ghastly fish genes but rather melded with sunny daffodils. But before we embrace genetic engineering as the saviour of the world's poor, it seems wise to sort out what problem is being solved here. Is it the crisis of malnutrition, or is it the crisis of credibility plaguing biotech?

The boring truth is that we already have the tools to save many more than a million kids a year—all without irrevocably changing the genetic makeup of food staples. What we lack is the political will to mobilize those resources. That was the clear message that emerged from the recent Group of Eight summit in Okinawa. One after another, the largest industrial nations shot down concrete proposals aimed at reducing poverty in the developing world. As *The Globe and Mail* reported, they nixed "a Canadian proposal to boost development aid by up to 10 percent, turned down Japan's idea to set up a G8 fund to fight infectious diseases, and backed away from opening their markets to farm goods from developing countries within four years." They also "said no to a new plan to accelerate US$100 billion in debt relief for the poorest countries." [*Even more telling was the June 2002 summit of the UN Food and Agriculture Organization in Rome. The ambitious goal of the gathering was to reduce the number of hungry people by half; from 800 million to 400 million by 2015. Yet of the 29 richest countries, only two sent their heads of state to Rome, and one of those was Italy, whose leader was already in town.*]

There are also plenty of low-tech solutions to vitamin A deficiency that have been similarly passed over. Programs already exist to encourage the growth of diverse, vitamin-rich vegetables on small plots, yet the irony of these programs (which receive little international support) is that their task is not to invent a sexy new sci-fi food source. It's to undo some of the damage created the last time Western companies and governments sold an agricultural panacea to the developing world.

During the so-called Green Revolution, small-scale peasant farmers, growing a wide variety of crops to feed their families and local communities, were pushed to shift to industrial, export-oriented agriculture. That meant single, high-yield crops, produced on a large scale. Many peasants, now at the mercy of volatile commodity prices and deep in debt to the seed companies, lost their farms and headed for the cities. In the countryside, meanwhile, severe malnutrition exists alongside flourishing "cash crops" such as bananas, coffee and rice. Why? Because in children's diets, as in the farm fields, diverse foods have been replaced with monotony. A bowl of white rice is lunch and dinner.

The solution being proposed by the agribusiness giants? Not to rethink mono-crop farming and fill that bowl with protein and vitamins. They want to wave another magic wand and paint the white bowl golden.

Genetic Pollution
With tampered seeds blowing from one field to the next, soon it will be impossible for any food to be labelled "GMO-Free"

June 2001

In the aisles of the giant supermarket Loblaws, between bottles of President's Choice Memories of Kobe sauce and Memories of Singapore noodles, there is a new in-store special: blacked-out labels on organic foods. These boxes used to say "Free of genetically modified organisms," but then Canada's largest grocery chain decreed that such labels were no longer permitted.

At first glance, its decision doesn't seem to make market sense. When the first Frankenfood protests came to Europe, chains such as Tesco and Safeway scrambled to satisfy consumer demand by labelling their own lines GMO-free. And when Loblaws entered the health food market with its line of President's Choice Organics, it seemed to be going the same route. In ads, the company proudly pointed out that certified organic products "must be free of genetically modified organisms."

Then the about-face, made public last week: not only will Loblaws not make the GMO-free claim on its own packages, it won't allow anyone else to make the claim. Company executives say there is just no way of knowing what's genuinely GMO-free—apparently it's too confusing.

More than 90 percent of Canadians tell pollsters they want labels indicating if their food's genetic makeup has been tampered with, but Galen Weston, chairman of Loblaw Companies, has publicly warned that "there will be a cost associated" with such an initiative. This, in part, explains the obliterating magic markers: if Loblaws carries organic products labelled GMO-free, it's harder to explain why the firm isn't informing consumers when food *does* contain genetically modified ingredients, as is the case for roughly 70 percent of Canadian foods. So the grocer has made a rather brutal choice: rather than give consumers some of the information they are demanding, it will provide none of it.

And this is only one salvo in a war being waged by the agribusiness industry on consumer choice in the genetic engineering debate—not just in Canada but potentially around the world. Faced with thirty-five countries that have developed, or are developing, mandatory GM labelling laws, the industry seems to be doing everything it can to make those European and Asian labels as obsolete as the ones that have been scratched out at Loblaws. How? By polluting faster than countries can legislate.

For example, one of the companies forced to remove its labels is Nature's Path, an organic food firm based in Delta, British Columbia. Earlier this month, company president Arran Stephens told *The New York Times* that GM material is indeed finding its way into organic crops. "We have found traces in corn that has been grown organically for ten to fifteen years. There's no wall high enough to keep that stuff contained."

Some organic food companies are considering suing the biotech industry for contamination, but the law is going in the opposite direction. Saskatchewan farmer Percy Schmeiser was sued by Monsanto after its patented genetically altered canola seeds blew into the farmer's field from passing trucks and neighbouring fields. Monsanto says that when the airborne seeds took root, Schmeiser was stealing its property. The court agreed and, two months ago, ordered the farmer to pay the company $20,000, plus legal costs.

The most well-known contamination case is StarLink corn. After the genetically altered crop (meant for animals and deemed unfit for humans) made its way into the food supply, Aventis, which owns the patent, proposed a solution: instead of recalling the corn, why not approve its consumption for humans? In other words, change the law to fit the contamination.

Around the world, consumers are exercising a renewed political power, demanding organic options at the supermarket and asking their governments for clear labelling of GM foods. Yet all the while, the agribusiness giants—backed by predatory intellectual property laws—are getting the global food supply so hopelessly cross-pollinated, contaminated, polluted and mixed up that legislators may well be forced to throw up their hands. As biotech critic Jeremy Rifkin says, "They're hoping there's enough contamination so that it's a *fait accompli*."

When we look back on this moment, munching our genetically modified Natural Values™ health-style food, our human-approved StarLink tacos and our mutated, farmed

Atlantic salmon, we may well remember it as the precise point when we lost our real food options. Perhaps Loblaws will even launch a new product to bottle that wistful feeling: Memories of Consumer Choice.

Foot-and-Mouth's Sacrificial Lambs
The primary goal of Europe's livestock slaughter is saving markets, not protecting public health

March 2001

The Taliban destroys two-thousand-year-old Buddha statues and we rightly shake our heads: how barbaric in these modern times to sacrifice graven images at the altar of religious purity. And yet, while Buddhas are bombed in Afghanistan, the European Union is engaged in its own quasi-biblical cleansing ritual: the fiery sacrifice of tens of thousands of animals to appease the hungry gods of free market economics. When I first heard the farm animals described as capital's sacrificial lambs (it was German environmentalist Mathias Greffrath who said it to me), I thought it was hyperbole. Surely those hillsides were burning to protect public health, not the market value of meat or future access to foreign markets.

More than fifty thousand animals are being or have already been killed in Britain, with another ten thousand marked for death. In Germany, where I've been visiting this week, fifteen hundred sheep have been destroyed. There was no evidence of infection—simply a chance that the animals might have come in contact with foot-and-mouth disease.

Some of this, of course, has to do with health. But not all of it. Foot-and-mouth disease is of little health risk to humans, and we can't get it through food. The disease can be cured quickly in animals with proper medicines and quarantines, then prevented with vaccination. Where the virus takes its true toll is on the market. And the market demands grand gestures to restore faith in its systems.

And make no mistake: a system is on trial in Europe's latest food scare. When a highly contagious virus such as foot-and-mouth enters the food chain, it forces consumers to think about how our food gets to the table. Polite phrases such as "integration," "homogenization" and "high intensity farming" suddenly take on graphic meaning.

The process of assessing the safety of each bite rudely yanks back the curtain of packaging and exposes massive factory farms and abattoirs, huge warehouses, the mega-chain supermarkets and fast-food outlets and the long distances that animals and meat travel in crowded trucks and boats in between each of these links in the industrial farming chain.

It increasingly seems that what is on trial in Europe is the tyranny of "economies of scale" that governs every aspect of food production, distribution and consumption. In each of these areas, the players follow the familiar formula of lowering their costs by consolidating and expanding operations, then using their clout to press suppliers to meet their terms. Not only does this recipe hurt small farmers and cut down on the variety of foods available, it's also a time bomb when it comes to disease. Concentration means viruses spread quickly through large numbers of animals, while globalization ensures they are carried far and wide.

Which is why Germany's agricultural minister is talking about new subsidies to help 20 percent of the country's farms become organic. And why British Prime Minister Tony Blair is making noises about loosening the grip of the big supermarket chains. It's also why those hoping to barrel ahead with genetically modified foods are no doubt watching all this with dismay.

This latest food scare could well be the decisive opportunity that campaigners against genetic modification have been waiting for. After all, the most immediate danger posed by GM crops is the way that altered seeds are carried by the wind, mixing with unaltered ones. Yet it has been tough to get the public interested in this subtle and invisible threat to biodiversity. That's why groups such as Greenpeace have tended to focus their campaigns more on potential dangers to public health, which, though more accessible, are less scientific.

But foot-and-mouth disease, which is spread through the air, now has much of Europe thinking about microbes and wind, about how interconnected the food supply is, how difficult it is to control any particle, no matter how small, once it has entered the system. "So be a vegetarian," some are saying. "Go organic." *The Financial Times* editors insist that "phasing out intensive agriculture is too glib an answer" and propose more "consumer choice." Somehow I doubt that Europe's food safety crisis will be solved this time with more organic niche marketing. After more than a decade of debates about mad cow disease, E. coli, GMOs and now foot-and-mouth, food safety is ceasing to be a health issue, or a consumer issue, and becoming an economic issue, one questioning the most basic bigger-is-better assumptions of industrial agriculture.

It's about shaken faith—in science, in industry, in politics, in experts. The markets may be satisfied with their sacrificial lambs, but I think the public may demand more lasting measures.

The Internet as Tupperware Party
How media giants are trying to own on-line file sharing

November 2000

When the top two executives at the New York–based music company BMG Entertainment resigned on the weekend, it revealed a deep schism in the way multinational companies see the Internet's culture of sharing. Despite all the attempts to turn the Net into a giant shopping mall, the default ethos still seems to be anti-shopping: on the Internet, we may purchase things here and there, but we share ceaselessly—ideas, humour, information and, yes, music files.

So here's the real debate as it goes down in the boardroom: is this culture of on-line swapping and trading a threat to the heart of the profit motive, or is it an unprecedented profit-making opportunity, a chance to turn sharing itself into an enormously profitable sales tool?

When the five major record labels, under the umbrella of the Recording Industry Association of America, launched a lawsuit against Napster, the music file-sharing site, they threw their lot decidedly into the first camp: file sharing is theft of copyright, pure and simple, and it must be stopped.

But last week, something strange happened: Bertelsmann, owner of BMG Entertainment (one of the five companies behind the RIAA lawsuit), struck a deal with Napster (hence the BMG resignations). The two companies are going to launch a file-sharing site where music fans pay a membership fee in exchange for access to BMG music. Once it's off the ground, Bertelsmann will pull out of the lawsuit. At the press conference, Thomas Middelhoff, chairman and chief executive of Bertelsmann, pitted himself against the suits over at Time Warner and Sony who just don't get the Net. "This is a call for the industry to wake up," he said.

So what's going on? Has Bertelsmann, a US$17.6 billion media conglomerate (which owns my Canadian publisher and pretty much everyone else's), decided to join the cyber-hippies who chant that "information wants to be free"? I somehow doubt it. More likely, Bertelsmann knows what more and more corporations understand: that after many failed attempts to use the Net as a direct sales tool, it may just turn out that the process of trading information is the Net's ultimate commercial use.

Napster defenders argue that they don't pirate CDs but rather swap music within an on-line community the way communities of friends swap mix tapes. They get to know and trust one another's taste and, they argue, they end up buying more music because they are exposed to more of it. They also say they have been driven to create this alternative by inflated CD prices and the hideously homogenous rotation of pop on video stations and commercial radio.

What's taking place on sites such as Napster is a high-tech version of something very old: people talking to other people directly about what they like. It used to be called "word of mouth"; in the Internet age, it's called "word of mouse." It's the X factor that can create a true phenomenon—such as *The Blair Witch Project*—and that marketers can't seem to purchase or control—witness the *Blair Witch* sequel.

Or can they? Trying to understand, systematize and harness this most human of all behaviours (how and why we talk to each other) has become something of a corporate obsession. Books such as *The Tipping Point* by Malcolm Gladwell, *The Anatomy of Buzz* by Emanuel Rosen and *Unleashing the Ideavirus* by Seth Godin offer quasi-scientific explanations for how ideas spread: less by advertising than by regular people who are respected by their peers. Gladwell calls them "connectors" and "mavens," Godin "sneezers" and Rosen "network hubs."

Based on this theory, a marketing school has developed that encourages companies to treat consumers as if they were journalists or celebrities: Feed them free stuff and watch them do your marketing for you, gratis. Put more bluntly, transform the ultimate anti-commodity—human communication, between friends, inside communities of trust—into a commercial transaction.

This is the irony of the record industry's crackdown on Napster. At the same time as the legal arms of record companies are pummelling file-sharing sites, their marketing arms are embracing these same on-line communities for their "peer-on-peer" potential. They've been paying firms such as ElectricArtists to strategically circulate free music samples and video clips in the hope of turning music fans into battalions of unpaid cyber Avon Ladies.

Bertelsmann itself used these techniques of "on-line seeding" to launch BMG artist Christina Aguilera: Electic-Artists gave away music samples to chatty Britney Spears fans, who then bombarded their on-line friends with the great news: she's been cloned!

When Bertelsmann made a deal with Napster last week, they were betting on a future in which sharing—when carefully controlled by marketers—is the Internet's "killer app": a global network of on-line brand-babble where authentic communities used to be.

The Internet as a giant Tupperware party. Are you ready?

Co-opting Dissent
How multinationals are "re-branding" for the post-Seattle era

May 2001

When I was seventeen, I worked after school at an Esprit clothing store in Montreal. It was a pleasant job, mostly involving folding cotton garments into little squares so sharp that their corners could take your eye out. But for some reason, corporate headquarters didn't consider our T-shirt origami to be sufficiently profitable. One day, our calm world was turned upside down by a regional supervisor who swooped in to indoctrinate us in the culture of the Esprit brand—and increase our productivity in the process. "Esprit," she told us, "is like a good friend."

I was skeptical, and I let it be known. Skepticism, I quickly learned, is not considered an asset in the low-wage service sector. Two weeks later, the supervisor fired me for being in possession of that most loathed workplace character trait: "bad attitude." I guess that was one of my first lessons in why large multinational corporations are not "like a good friend," since good friends, while they may sometimes do horrible and hurtful things, rarely fire you.

So I was interested when, earlier this month, the TBWA/Chiat/Day advertising agency rolled out the new "brand identity" for Shoppers Drug Mart. (Rebranding launches are, in corporate terms, like being born again.) It turns out that the chain is no longer Everything You Want in a Drugstore—i.e., a place where you can buy things you need; it too is now a "caring friend," one that takes form as a chain of eight hundred drugstores with a $22 million ad budget burning a hole in its pocket.

Shoppers' new slogan is Take Care of Yourself, selected, according to campaign creator Pat Pirisi because it echoes "what a caring friend would say." Get ready for it to be said thousands of times a day by young cashiers as they hand you plastic bags filled with razors, dental floss and diet pills. "We believe this is a position Shoppers can own," Pirisi says.

Asking clerks to adopt this particular phrase as their mantra seems a bit heartless in this age of casual, insecure, underpaid McLabour. Service-sector workers are so often told to take care of themselves—since no one, least of all their mega-employers, is going to take care of them.

Yet it's one of the ironies of our branded age that as corporations become more remote by cutting lasting ties with us as their employees, they are increasingly sidling up to us as consumers, whispering sweet nothings in our ear about friendship and community. It's not just Shoppers: Wal-Mart ads tell stories about clerks who, in a pinch, lend customers their own wedding gowns, and Saturn ads are populated by car dealers who offer counselling when customers lose their jobs. You see, according to a new marketing book, *Values Added,* modern marketers have to "make your brand a cause and your cause a brand."

Maybe I still have a bad attitude, but this collective

corporate hug feels about as empty today as it did when I was an about-to-be-unemployed sweater folder. Particularly when you stop to consider the cause of all this mass-produced warmth.

Explaining Shoppers' new brand identity to *The Financial Post*, Pirisi said, "In an age when people are becoming more and more distrustful of corporations—the World Trade Organization protests will attest to that—and at a time when the health care system isn't what it used to be, we realized we had to send consumers a message about partnership."

Ever since large corporations such as Nike, Shell and Monsanto began facing increased scrutiny from civil society—mostly for putting short-term profits far ahead of environmental responsibility and job security—an industry has ballooned to help these companies respond. It seems clear, however, that many in the corporate world remain utterly convinced that all they have is a "messaging problem," one that can be neatly solved by settling on the right, socially minded brand identity.

It turns out that's the last thing they need. British Petroleum found this out the hard way when it was forced to distance itself from its own outrageous rebranding campaign, Beyond Petroleum. Understandably, many consumers interpreted the new slogan to mean the company was moving away from fossil fuels in response to climate change. Human rights and environmental activists, after seeing no evidence that BP was actually changing its policies, brought up embarrassing details at the company's annual meeting about BP's participation in a controversial new pipeline through sensitive areas of Tibet, as well as its decision to drill in the Alaska National Wildlife Refuge. With the new slogan being parodied on the Net as Beyond Preposterous, BP officials moved to abandon the Beyond Petroleum brand, though they have so far stuck with the new green flower logo.

As evidence of the state of corporate confusion, I frequently find myself asked to give presentations to individual corporations. Fearing that my words will end up in some gooey ad campaign, I always refuse. But I can offer this advice without reservation: nothing will change until corporations realize that they don't have a communications problem. They have a reality problem.

Economic Apartheid in South Africa
After the fight for freedom has been won, racial divisions are being replaced by new systems of exclusion

November 2001

On Saturday night, I found myself at a party honouring Nelson Mandela and raising money for his children's fund. It was a lovely affair, and only a very rude person would have pointed out that the party was packed with many of the banking and mining executives who had refused to pull their investments out of apartheid-run South Africa for decades.

Similarly, only someone with no sense of timing would have mentioned that as our government was making Mandela an honorary Canadian citizen, it was also trying to ram through an anti-terrorism bill that would have sabotaged the anti-apartheid movement on several fronts had it been in place at the time.

The Canadian anti-apartheid movement raised money for the African National Congress, which would easily have fitted Bill C-36's sloppy definition of a terrorist organization. Furthermore, anti-apartheid activists deliberately caused "serious disruption" to companies that invested in South Africa, eventually forcing many to pull out. These disruptions would also have been illegal under C-36.

Only someone with absolutely no sense of propriety would have muttered, amid all the self-congratulation, that many in South Africa insist that apartheid still exists and requires a new resistance movement. But two weeks ago, I met Trevor Ngwane, a former ANC municipal council member, who says just that. "Apartheid based on race has been replaced with apartheid based on class."

Confronted with a country where eight million people are homeless and nearly five million are HIV positive, some try to paint deep inequality as a sad but unavoidable legacy of racial apartheid. Ngwane says it is the direct result of a specific economic "restructuring" program, embraced by the current government and nurtured by the World Bank and the International Monetary Fund.

When Mandela was freed from prison, his vision was of a South Africa that offered economic, as well as democratic, freedom. Basic needs for housing, water and electricity would be met through massive public works programs. But as power came into the ANC's reach, writes South African professor Patrick Bond in his new book, *Against Global Apartheid*, enormous pressure was put on the party to prove it could govern with "sound macroeconomic policies." It became clear that if Mandela attempted genuine redistribution of wealth, the international markets would punish South Africa. Many within the party understandably feared that an economic meltdown would be used as an indictment not just of the ANC but of black rule itself.

[*Their fears were confirmed more recently. In July 2002, the ANC was set to pass a new law that would diversify*

access to South Africa's enormous mineral wealth, now con-
centrated in the hands of a few white-owned mining multi-
nationals. The big mining investors rebelled against the plan
and threatened to withdraw from the country. Jonathan
Oppenheimer, head of public relations for the diamonds
giant De Beers, said the law "would put a line through
South Africa as an investment destination."]

So instead of its policy of "growth through redistribution," the ANC, particularly under President Thabo Mbeki,
adopted the cookie-cutter free-trade program: trying to
"grow" the economy by pleasing foreign investors through
mass privatizations, layoffs and wage cuts in the public sector, corporate tax cuts and the like.

The results have been devastating. Half a million jobs have
been lost since 1993. Wages for the poorest 40 percent
have dropped by 21 percent. Poor areas have seen their
water costs go up by 55 percent, electricity by as much as
400 percent. Many have resorted to drinking polluted water,
leading to a cholera outbreak that infected 100,000 people.
In Soweto, twenty thousand homes have their electricity cut
off each month. And the investment? They're still waiting.

This is the type of track record that has turned the
World Bank and the IMF into international pariahs, drawing thousands to the streets of Ottawa last weekend, with
a "solidarity protest" in Johannesburg. *The Washington Post*
recently told the heartbreaking story of one Soweto resi-
dent, Agnes Mohapi. The reporter observed, "For all its
wretchedness, apartheid never did this: It did not lay her off
from her job, jack up her utility bill, then disconnect her

service when she inevitably could not pay. 'Privatization did that,' she said."

In the face of this system of "economic apartheid," a new resistance movement is inevitable. There was a three-day general strike against privatization in August. (Workers held up signs that read, "ANC We Love You But Not Privatizations.") In Soweto, unemployed workers reconnect their neighbours' cut-off water, and the Soweto Electricity Crisis Committee has illegally reconnected power in thousands of homes. Why don't the police arrest them? "Because," Ngwane says, "when the police officers' electricity is disconnected, we reconnect them too."

It looks as if the corporate executives, so eager to have their pictures taken with Nelson Mandela last weekend, have a second chance to fight apartheid—this time while it's still going on. They can do it not only through good-hearted charity, but by questioning the economic logic that is failing so many around the world. Which side will they be on this time?

Poison Policies in Ontario
When basic needs are treated as commodities

June 2000

Just after noon tomorrow, a few hundred protesters, many of them homeless, will arrive on the steps of the Ontario Legislature with a very simple request. They want to speak to the Tory government about the effects its policies are having on the poor. If history has anything to teach us, Premier Mike Harris will make a get-tough speech about how Ontario's voters have made their voices heard and he won't be bullied—right before he calls in the cops for a smash-up. The question is, How will the rest of us react?

I ask this because since the E. coli outbreak in the town of Walkerton, in which more than two thousand residents fell ill from drinking the municipal water, voters across Ontario have been searching their souls about the effects of Tory deregulation on real people and their daily lives. There has been widespread horror at the possibility that government cuts to the Ministry of the Environment, and downloading to municipalities, may have put the people of Walkerton at great risk.

Public outrage is a powerful, transformative force, even in Mike Harris's seemingly impenetrable political enclave. This outrage has led directly to the convening of four inquiries into the causes of the water crisis, to political commitments to fix the problems identified, as well as an offer of millions of dollars in compensation. The tragedy deserves this swift attention and more. But why did we need the deaths in Walkerton to make us see that abstract policies take their toll on real people's lives?

Seven people, possibly more, died from drinking E. coli–infected water, and tomorrow the Ontario Coalition Against Poverty is marching on Queen's Park because twenty-two homeless people died on the streets of Toronto in the past seven months. The connections between those deaths and government cutbacks and deregulation are just as compelling in Toronto as they are in Walkerton. Perhaps even more so, because in Toronto we don't need four inquiries to establish the connections—they are virtually taken as a given.

Before the Tories were elected, some winters passed with absolutely no homeless deaths on the streets of Toronto. The death toll began to mount in 1995, the same year the Tories cut welfare by 21.6 percent and the same year they nixed plans for new social housing. Just after that, the economic recovery that the Tories love to take credit for began to drive rental rates way up, while the Tory Tenant Protection Act has made it much easier for landlords to throw out their renters. Roughly sixteen hundred renters now face eviction each month in Toronto.

The result is a staggering number of people on the streets and not enough beds for them in shelters. Last year, there were five thousand emergency hostel beds available in the city, but many social workers say there is demand for twice that many. As the hostels and streets become more crowded, street culture becomes more degraded and violent. And it is here that the Tories step in with their Safe Streets Act, a new measure that allows the police to treat homeless people like criminals, prime content-providers for Ontario's coming private super-jail.

Just as there are clear remedies available to prevent future Walkertons, there are plenty of obvious policy solutions to prevent future street deaths. More housing, better tenant protection and less harassment are all good places to start. Anti-poverty groups have put forward the "1 percent solution": a call to double the amount of money available for affordable housing by getting all levels of government to contribute an additional 1 percent of their total budgets.

In comparing the E. coli deaths in Walkerton to the homeless crisis in Toronto, I am not trying to pit one tragedy against another in some kind of misery sweepstakes, only pointing out that the debate about homelessness has two ingredients missing: noisy public outrage and the political will to prevent future tragedies.

This is Mike Harris's Ontario in action. The first lesson of the Tories' Common Sense Revolution [the campaign slogan on which they came to power] was that there are two clear classes of people in the province: those who are inside the system, and those who belong outside it. Those who are inside have been rewarded with tax cuts; those on the outside have been pushed farther out still.

The people of Walkerton were supposed to be on the inside: hard working, tax paying, healthy, Tory voting. The dead on the streets of Toronto were exiled from Day 1 of the Common Sense Revolution: unemployed, poor, mentally ill.

Only now the neat lines of the Tories' hierarchy of humanity are blurring. "The Harris agenda goes beyond destroying the social structure and has started to erode the very physical structure everyone relies upon," says John Clarke, spokesperson for the Ontario Coalition Against Poverty, the group organizing tomorrow's demonstration. "In the end, it becomes obvious that everyone is under attack."

America's Weakest Front
The public sector

October 2001

Only hours after the terrorist attacks on the World Trade Center and the Pentagon, Republican Congressman Curt Weldon went on CNN and announced that he didn't want to hear anyone talking about funding for schools or hospitals. From here on, it was all about spies, bombs and other manly things. "The first priority of the U.S. government is not education, it is not health care, it is the defence and protection of U.S. citizens," he said, adding, later, "I'm a teacher married to a nurse—none of that matters today."

But now it turns out that those frivolous social services matter a great deal. What is making the U.S. most vulnerable to terrorist networks is not a depleted weapons arsenal but its starved, devalued and crumbling public sector. The new battlefields are not just the Pentagon but also the post office; not just military intelligence but also training for doctors and nurses; not a sexy new missile defence shield but the boring old Food and Drug Administration.

It has become fashionable to wryly observe that the terrorists use the West's technologies as weapons against itself: planes, e-mail, cellphones. But as fears of bioterrorism mount, it could well turn out that their best weapons are the rips and holes in the United States' public infrastructure.

Is this because there was no time to prepare for the

attacks? Hardly. The U.S. has openly recognized the threat of biological attacks since the Persian Gulf war, and Bill Clinton renewed calls to protect the nation from bioterror after the 1998 embassy bombings in East Africa. And yet shockingly little has been done.

The reason is simple: preparing for biological warfare would have required a ceasefire in America's older, less dramatic war—the one against the public sphere. It didn't happen. Here are some snapshots from the front lines.

Half the states in the U.S. don't have federal experts trained in bioterrorism. The Centers for Disease Control and Prevention are buckling under the strain of anthrax fears, their underfunded labs scrambling to keep up with the demand for tests. Little research has been done on how to treat children who have contracted anthrax, since Cipro—the most popular antibiotic—is not recommended for them.

Many doctors in the U.S. public health care system have not been trained to identify symptoms of anthrax, botulism or plague. A recent U.S. Senate panel heard that hospitals and health departments lack basic diagnostic tools, and information sharing is difficult since some departments don't have e-mail access. Many health departments are closed on weekends, with no staff on call.

If treatment is a mess, federal inoculation programs are in worse shape. The only laboratory in the U.S. licensed to produce the anthrax vaccine has left the country unprepared for its current crisis. Why? It's a typical privatization debacle. The lab, in Lansing, Michigan, used to be owned and operated by the state. In 1998, it was sold to BioPort, which promised greater efficiency. The new lab has failed several FDA inspections and, so far, has been unable to supply a single dose of the vaccine to the U.S. military, let alone to the general population.

As for smallpox, there are not nearly enough vaccines to cover the population, leading the U.S. National Institute of Allergy and Infectious Diseases to experiment with diluting the existing vaccines at a ratio of 1 to 5 or even 1 to 10.

Internal documents show that the U.S. Environmental Protection Agency is years behind schedule in safeguarding the water supply against bioterrorist attacks. According to an audit released on October 4, the EPA was supposed to have identified security vulnerabilities in municipal water supplies by 1999, but it hasn't yet completed even this first stage.

The FDA has proven unable to introduce measures that would better protect the food supply from "agroterrorism"— deadly bacteria introduced into the food supply. With agriculture increasingly centralized and globalized, the sector is vulnerable to the spread of disease. But the FDA, which inspected only 1 percent of food imports under its jurisdiction last year, says it is in "desperate need of more inspectors."

Tom Hammonds, CEO of the Food Marketing Institute, an industry group representing food sellers, says, "Should a crisis arise—real or manufactured as a hoax—the deficiencies of the current system would become glaringly obvious."

After September 11, George W. Bush created the office of "homeland security," designed to evoke a nation steeled and prepared for any attack. And yet it turns out that what "homeland security" really means is a mad rush to reassemble basic public infrastructure and resurrect health and safety standards that have been drastically eroded. The troops at the front lines of America's new war are embattled indeed: they are the very bureaucracies that have been cut back, privatized and vilified for two decades, not just in the U.S. but in virtually every country in the world.

"Public health is a national security issue," U.S. Secretary of Health Tommy Thompson observed earlier this month. No kidding. For years, critics have argued that there are human costs to all the cost-cutting, deregulating and privatizing— train crashes in Britain, E. coli outbreaks in Walkerton, food poisoning, street deaths and substandard health care. And yet until September 11, "security" was still narrowly confined to the machinery of war and policing, a fortress built atop a crumbling foundation.

If there is a lesson to be learned, it is that real security cannot be cordoned off. It is woven into our most basic social fabric, from the post office to the emergency room, from the subway to the water reservoir, from schools to food inspection. Infrastructure—the boring stuff that binds us all together—is not irrelevant to the serious business of fighting terrorism. It is the foundation of our future security.

III

FENCING IN THE MOVEMENT: CRIMINALIZING DISSENT

In which copious quantities of gas are inhaled, friends are thrown into vans by cops dressed as anarchists, and a boy dies in Genoa

III

FENCING IN THE MOVEMENT: CRIMINALIZING DISSENT

In which copious quantities of gas are inhaled, friends are thrown into vans by cops dressed as anarchists, and a boy dies in Genoa

Cross-Border Policing
Law enforcement officials swap intimidation tricks

May 2000

"We have learned the lessons of Seattle and Washington," RCMP Constable Michèle Paradis tells me on the cellphone from Windsor. She is in charge of media relations for the meeting of the Organization of American States that is coming to Windsor, Ontario, this weekend, where she will be joined by a few thousand protesters who object to the OAS's plans to expand NAFTA into all of Latin America and the Caribbean.

"And what were those lessons?" I ask.

"I'm afraid I can't answer that," she says.

This is unfortunate, because there are any number of lessons that the Canadian police could have learned about how to treat protesters in the wake of the demonstrations against the World Trade Organization in Seattle and the demonstrations against the World Bank and International Monetary Fund in Washington, D.C. In the absence of any elaboration from Constable Paradis, here are the key lessons the Mounties *appear* to have learned from their colleagues to the south.

LESSON #1: STRIKE PRE-EMPTIVELY

Local activists in Windsor say they have been getting phone

calls and home visits from Royal Canadian Mounted Police officers. Josie Hazen, a graphic designer who produced a poster advertising the rally and teach-in put on by the Canadian Labour Congress, says an RCMP officer contacted her and asked a series of questions about these perfectly legal events, its organizers and her knowledge of other anti-OAS activities. "Lots of people have been getting these calls and we think it's a scare tactic to keep us away from the protests," Hazen says.

LESSON #2: NORMALIZE POLICE VIOLENCE

In Washington, I met several nineteen-year-old activists who carried the requisite protective gear of swimming goggles and bandanas soaked in vinegar. It's not that they were planning to attack a Starbucks, just that they've come to expect that getting gassed is what happens when you express your political views.

In Canada, when we saw university students being doused with pepper spray outside the 1997 Asia-Pacific Economic Cooperation summit in Vancouver, there was a wave of public outrage. Now, two and a half years later, we have seen so much brutality directed against protesters that we appear to have become used to it. And this is the truly insidious effect of police violence: if protesters are publicly treated like criminals regularly enough, they start to look like criminals, and we begin, albeit unconsciously, to equate activism with sinister wrongdoing, even terrorism.

LESSON #3: ERASE THE DISTINCTION BETWEEN CIVIL DISOBEDIENCE AND VIOLENCE

There is a faction going to Windsor that plans to practise civil disobedience, to put their bodies on the line to block access to parts of the OAS meeting. This is a tactic used by activists historically and around the world to protest against unjust laws. In North America, it came in handy during the civil rights movement, the anti-Vietnam War protests and, more recently, in native blockades, labour disputes and the 1993 standoff between environmentalists and loggers in Clayoquot Sound, off Canada's West Coast. It is not a violent tactic—but it is designed to be an inconvenient one.

Essentially, what the protesters are planning for the OAS meeting in Windsor is a sit-in on the streets. Though this may annoy people trying to get to work, sometimes—when meaningful avenues for public expression have been exhausted—important political victories are won out of the small inconveniences.

Yet when I spoke to Constable Paradis she repeatedly described the plans to shut down the Windsor meeting as "violence," refusing to recognize that blocking a road could be done peacefully. "That's semantics," she said of the distinction.

None of the organizers of the Windsor protests are endorsing violence, which brings us to:

LESSON #4: DIVIDE AND CONQUER

"We're not concerned with the peaceful protesters,"

Constable Paradis told me. "Just the minority bent on shutting things down." This distinction between good protesters—those only interested in shouting slogans and waving banners in sanctioned areas—and bad, direct-action protesters was also a constant police refrain in Seattle and Washington.

But the activists have learned some lessons of their own. Seattle showed that civil disobedience adds much needed urgency and attention to official marches and teach-ins, events usually ignored by a been-there-done-that press. So, in the run-up to Windsor, there is a virtual consensus among organizers that you don't have to choose between tactics—there can be hundreds of them, and activism can work on several complementary fronts at once.

The real irony in police attacks on anti-free-trade activists is that it comes in the midst of months of preaching about how increased trade with China will fill that country's citizenry with an irrepressible thirst for democracy and freedom of expression. The opposite is clearly true: this model of free trade is so damaging to so many people around the world that democratic countries are wilfully compromising the rights of their own citizens to protect the smooth advancement of its agenda.

Which brings us to Lesson #5, the one both police and politicians seem determined not to hear. In the era of corporate globalization, politics itself is becoming a gated community, with ever more security and brutality required for it to conduct business as usual.

Pre-emptive Arrest
Police target puppet master in Windsor, Ontario

June 2000

"This is David Solnit. He's the Man."

That's how the legendary activist from San Francisco was introduced to me last Friday. We were at the University of Windsor at the time, both giving speeches at a teach-in on the Organization of American States. Of course, I already knew that David Solnit was the Man. He was one of the organizers of the shutdown in Seattle. And I have been hearing his name for years, usually spoken with reverence by young activists who have just attended one of his Art and Revolution workshops.

They come back brimming with new ideas about protests. How the demonstrations shouldn't be quasi-militaristic marches culminating in placard waving outside locked government buildings. How, instead, they should be "festivals of resistance," filled with giant puppets and theatrical spontaneity. How their goals should be more than symbolic: protests can "reclaim" public space for a party or a garden, or stop a planned meeting the protesters believe is destructive. This is the "show don't tell" theory that holds that you don't change minds just by screaming about what you are against. You change minds by building organizations and events that are a living example of what you stand for.

As I'm not schooled in this theory myself, my speech to

the students was a straight-up lecture about how the protests against an expanded free trade agreement for the Americas are part of a broader anti-corporate movement—against growing corporate control over education, water, scientific research and more.

When it was David Solnit's turn, he asked everybody to stand, turn to the next person, and ask them why they were here. As a child of hippie parents and a survivor of alternative summer camps, these instant-intimacy rituals have always made me want to run to my room and slam the door. Of course, David Solnit had to choose me as his partner— and he wasn't satisfied with "I came to give a speech." So I told him more: how writing about the commitment of young human rights and environmental activists gives me hope for the future and is a much needed antidote to the atmosphere of cynicism in which journalists are so immersed.

It wasn't until we had to share our discoveries with the room that I realized this wasn't just a get-to-know-you game: it was also an effective way to torment barely under-cover police officers. "Yeah, uh, my partner's name's Dave and he's here to fight oppression," said a guy in a nylon jacket and buzz cut.

Less than twenty-four hours later, David Solnit was in a Windsor jail cell, where he stayed for four days.

The day after the teach-in—which was the day before the large demonstration against the OAS—Solnit led a small puppet-making workshop at the university. After the seminar, only a block away from the campus, the police pulled him over. They said he had been convicted of crimes in the

United States and was thus considered a criminal in Canada. Why? Because fifteen years ago he was arrested at a protest against U.S. military involvement in Central America; he had written (in washable paint) the names of executed Sandinistas on the wall of a government building. Yesterday, after the protesters had already gone home, an Immigration Review Board inquiry found that Solnit's arrest was wholly unfounded, and he was released.

David Solnit preaches revolution through papier-mâché, which makes it tempting to dismiss the police's actions as raving paranoia. Except that the authorities are right to see him as a threat—though not to anyone's safety or property. His message is consistently non-violent, but it is also extremely powerful.

Solnit doesn't talk much about how free trade agreements turn culture, water, seeds and even genes into tradeable commodities. What he does in his workshops is teach young activists how to decommodify their relationships with one another—an original message for a generation that grew up being targeted by ads in their school washrooms and sold canned rebellion by soft drink companies.

Though Solnit was locked away until the OAS meetings had concluded, his ideas were all over Windsor: art was not something made by experts and purchased by consumers, it was everywhere on the streets. Activists even developed a free transportation system: a battalion of "blue bikes"—old bikes repaired and painted for protesters to use at their discretion.

Communications theorist Neil Postman once wrote that teaching is a "subversive activity." When teaching puts young people in touch with powers of self-sufficiency and creativity they didn't know they had, it is indeed subversive. But it is not criminal.

David Solnit was the object of a well-planned, cross-border police operation. He was identified as a political threat before he arrived in this country. His past was researched, he was followed, then arrested on trumped-up charges. All Canadians should be ashamed of the actions of our police. But most ashamed should be the trade bureaucrats in Windsor. It seems there is still one aspect of human life not covered by free trade: the free trade of empowering ideas.

Surveillance
It's easier to spy on activists than engage them in open debate

August 2000

I wasn't thrilled that the Canadian Security Intelligence Service quoted my book in its new report on the anti-globalization threat. In some of the circles I travel in, writing for *The Globe and Mail* is enough of a political liability, never mind being a de facto CSIS informant. But there it is on page 3 of the report: *No Logo* helping CSIS to understand why those crazy kids keep storming trade meetings.

Usually, I welcome any and all readers, but I have this sneaking suspicion that next April, this report will be used to justify smashing in the heads of some good friends of mine. That's when Quebec City will play host to the Summit of the Americas, the most significant free trade meeting since the World Trade Organization negotiations collapsed in Seattle last December.

The CSIS report was designed to assess the threat that anti-corporate protests posed to the summit. But, interestingly, it does more than paint activists as latent terrorists (though it does that, too). It also makes a somewhat valiant effort to understand the issues behind the anger.

The report notes, for instance, that protesters are enraged by "the failure to approve debt relief for poor countries." They believe that many corporations are guilty of "social injustice, unfair labour practices . . . as well as lack of concern for the environment," and that the institutions governing trade are "interested only in the profit motive." It's not a bad summary, really—infiltrating all those teach-ins paid off. The report even pays the protesters a rare compliment: according to CSIS, they are "becoming more and more knowledgeable about their subject."

Undoubtedly, these observations are made in the spirit of know thine enemy, but at least CSIS is listening. Which is more than you can say for Canada's minister of International Trade. In an address to the Inter-American Development Bank this month, Pierre Pettigrew set out a bizarre George Lucas–style dynamic in which free traders are the forces of global order and its critics the forces of "global disorder." These sinister foes aren't motivated by "idealism"—as the CSIS report states—but are driven by a selfish desire "to exclude others from the kind of prosperity we enjoy." And they don't have legitimate concerns; according to Pettigrew, they don't have a clue. "Globalization, quite simply, is part of the natural evolutionary process," the minister said. "It goes hand in hand with the progress of humanity, something which history tells us no one can stand in the way of."

If the Canadian government is worried that protesters are going to ruin its party in Quebec City, it should start by admitting that Mother Nature doesn't write international trade agreements, politicians and bureaucrats do. Better yet, instead of "monitoring the communications of protesters," as the CSIS reports calls for, the Liberal government should drag the discussion out of the cloak-and-dagger domain of intelligence reports and devote the next eight months to an open, inclusive, national debate on whether there is majority support for a hemisphere-wide NAFTA.

There is a precedent. In 1988, the Liberals, as the centre-left party, played a leading role in just such a debate, over the free trade agreement with the U.S. But back then, the pros and cons of trade deregulation were theoretical: it was a war, essentially, of competing predictions.

Now, Canadians are in a position to examine the track record. We can ask ourselves, Have the NAFTA rulings allowed us to protect our culture over the past eight years? Has the labour-side agreement protected the rights of factory workers in Canada and Mexico? Has the environmental-side agreement given us the freedom to regulate polluters? Have human rights, from Chiapas to Los Angeles to Toronto, been strengthened since NAFTA was introduced?

We can also look at the proportion of our GDP that relies on trade (43 percent), at the standard of living for average Canadians (stagnant). Then we can ask ourselves, Is this the best economic system we can imagine? Are we satisfied with more of the same? Do we really want NAFTA x 34? Such debate in itself would be evidence of a healthy democracy, but we could go even further. Canada's entry in the FTAA could become a core issue in the next federal election and—here's a crazy idea—we could vote on it.

It won't happen, of course. Democracy in Canada will be relegated to a petty haggling over tax cuts. The critics of our economic path will become more disenfranchised and more militant. And the job of the police will be to protect our politicians from real politics, even if it means turning Quebec City into a fortress.

Setting the stage for this use of force, the CSIS report concludes that "given the virulent anti-globalization rhetoric . . . the threat of summit-associated violence in Quebec City cannot be ruled out." Perhaps it can't. But given the virulent anti-activist rhetoric, and the collusion of our politicians, the threat of police violence in Quebec City is virtually guaranteed.

Fear Mongering
Police make protest seem so scary, who would want to go?

March 2001

"I am worried that free trade is leading to the privatization of education," an elementary school teacher in Ottawa tells me. "I want to go to the protests in Quebec City, but is it going to be safe?"

"I think NAFTA has increased the divide between rich and poor," a young mother in Toronto says. "But if I go to Quebec, will my son get pepper-sprayed?"

"I want to go to Quebec City," a Harvard undergraduate active in the anti-sweatshop movement tells me, "but I heard no one is getting across the border."

"We're not even bothering to go to Quebec City," a student in Mexico City says. "We can't afford to get arrested in a foreign country."

If you think that the next big crackdown on political protest is going to take place when six thousand police officers clash with activists outside the Summit of the Americas in Quebec City next month, you are mistaken. The real crackdown is already taking place. It is happening silently, with no fanfare, every time another would-be demonstrator decides not to publicly express his or her views about the proposed Free Trade Area of the Americas.

It turns out that the most effective form of crowd control isn't pepper spray, water cannons, tear gas or any of the other weapons being readied by Quebec police in anticipation of the arrival of thirty-four heads of state. The most cutting-edge form of crowd control is controlling the crowds before they converge: this is state-of-the-art protest deterrence—the silencing you do yourself.

It happens every time we read another story about how Quebec will be surrounded by a three-metre-high fence. Or about how there's nowhere to sleep in the city except the prisons, which have been helpfully cleared out. A month before the summit, postcard-perfect Quebec City has been successfully transformed into a menacing place, inhospitable to regular people with serious concerns about corporate-driven trade and economic deregulation. Expressing dissent, rather than being a healthy part of democracy, is becoming an extreme and dangerous sport, suitable only for hard-core activists, with bizarre accessories and doctoral degrees in scaling buildings.

More dissent deterrence takes place when we accept the stories in the newspapers, filled with anonymous sources and unattributed statements, about how some of these activists are actually "agitators" who are "planning to use violence," packing bricks and explosives. The only proof provided for such inflammatory allegations is that "anarchists" are organizing into "small groups" and these groups are "autonomous," meaning they don't tell each other what to do.

The truth is this: not a single one of the official groups organizing protests in Quebec City is planning violent action.

A couple of the more radical organizations, including the Anti-Capitalist Convergence, have said they respect "a diversity of tactics . . . ranging from popular education to direct action." They have said they will not, on principle, condemn other activists for their tactics. Some say they will defend themselves if attacked by the police.

This admittedly complicated position has been distorted in newspapers as tantamount to planning violent attacks on the summit, which it most certainly is not. It's also a source of frustration for many other activists who argue that it would be easier if everyone just signed on to a statement saying the protests will be non-violent.

The problem is that one of the fundamental arguments against the FTAA's Darwinian economic model is that it increases violence: violence within poor communities and police violence against the poor. In a speech delivered last year, International Trade Minister Pierre Pettigrew helped explain why. In modern economies, he said, "the victims are not only exploited, they're excluded. . . . You may be in a situation where you are not needed to create that wealth. This phenomenon of exclusion is far more radical than the phenomenon of exploitation."

Indeed it is. Which is why a society that blithely accepts this included/excluded ledger is an unsafe society, filled with people who have little faith in the system, who feel they have nothing to gain from the promises of prosperity coming out of gatherings such as the Summit of the Americas, who see the police only as a force of repression, who have nothing to lose.

If this isn't the kind of society we want—one of included and excluded, and ever-higher fences dividing the two— then the answer is not for "good" activists to pre-emptively condemn "bad" activists. The answer is to reject the politics of division wholesale. And the best place to do it is in Quebec City, where the usually invisible wall of exclusion has been made starkly visible, with a new chain-link fence and crowd-control methods that aim to keep us out before we even get there.

The "Citizens Caged" Petition
An open letter to Jean Chrétien before the Summit of the Americas

April 2001

Naomi Klein, actor Sarah Polley, and lawyer Clayton Ruby initiated this petition to Canadian Prime Minister Jean Chrétien in anticipation of police violence during the Summit of the Americas in Quebec City. The letter sought to galvanize public opinion, particularly in the arts community. Over six thousand Canadians signed: artists, academics, journalists, judges, lawyers and intellectuals. Among them were some of Canada's most prominent cultural figures, including Margaret Atwood, Michael Ondaatje, Atom Egoyan, Michael Ignatieff, Rubin "Hurricane" Carter and the Barenaked Ladies.

As Canadians who value freedom of expression as an essential democratic right and depend on that right to make our living, we will watch with vigilance the actions of police officers and immigration agents next week when the Summit of the Americas convenes in Quebec City.

The right to freedom of expression, so fundamental to our democracy, includes the right not just to speak and communicate but to be heard. The constitutional right to peaceful assembly encompasses the right to gather in public spaces in all Canadian cities. The right to freedom of movement across borders extends not just to trade and tourism but also to political rallies, conferences and protests.

Designed to keep lawful protesters out of sight and earshot, the security barrier constructed around Quebec City tramples on such fundamental freedoms. Following the spirit of our constitution, we condemn this action. We believe that the planned presence of approximately six thousand police officers around the summit site is not an incentive to peaceful protest. We also condemn the practice of arbitrarily refusing entry to concerned citizens of other countries, thereby preventing them from expressing their views to the world media about a free trade agreement that extends across thirty-four national borders.

Democracy does not only take place in parliaments, voting booths and official summits. It takes place in meeting halls, public parks and in the streets. It also includes, at times, peaceful acts of civil disobedience. When the streets are blocked off and hundreds of meeting halls in Quebec City are out of reach to citizens because they are inside a sprawling "security zone," it is democracy itself that is marginalized. And when large corporations are given the opportunity to buy access to political leaders through partial sponsorship of the Summit of the Americas, as has transpired here, it creates the impression that political accountability is for sale.

We are also concerned about leaked Canadian Security Intelligence Service documents that portray protesters coming to Quebec City as "violent," yet fail to support that claim with any corroborating evidence; and that such unsupported characterizations, repeated in press reports, could set the stage for excessive use of force by police officers. Many of the activists headed for Quebec City are young people expressing their political views and engaged in principled and peaceful expression and civil disobedience, and we are gravely concerned about all the protesters' physical safety.

In the past four years, we have watched the use of pepper spray become distressingly commonplace at political demonstrations timed with meetings of the World Bank, the International Monetary Fund, the World Trade Organization, the World Economic Forum, the Asia Pacific Economic Co-operation forum, as well as U.S. political conventions. We have also witnessed, from the streets of Washington, D.C., to Davos, Switzerland, the escalating use of tear gas, mass arrests, water cannons and rubber bullets by police during some of these demonstrations, as well as such increasingly common security techniques as pre-emptive arrests of protest organizers, random beatings of activists, raids on activist "convergence centres" and the seizure of harmless protest materials such as placards and puppets.

Throughout this country's history, Canadians such as George Étienne Cartier and Robert Baldwin have fought for both civic tolerance and the democratic right of freedom of expression. It is not too late for the Summit of the Americas to be an event during which our political leaders do more than talk about democracy. They can also embody demo-cratic principles of freedom of expression and movement by refusing to shield themselves from open criticism and debate on matters of crucial importance to citizens of the Americas. With the world watching closely, this is an opportunity to make Canada a model for democratic principles.

In this spirit, we call on the security forces at our borders and in Quebec City to vigorously defend not only the safety of visiting heads of state but the rights of political activists within Canada.

Infiltration

Plainclothes cops nab peaceful organizer at Free Trade Area of the Americas protest

April 2001

"Where are you?" I screamed from my cellphone into his.

There was a pause and then, "A Green Zone—St. Jean and St. Claire."

Green Zone is protest speak for an area free of tear gas or police clashes. There are no fences to storm, only sanctioned marches. Green Zones are safe; you're supposed to be able to bring your kids to them. "Okay," I said. "See you in fifteen minutes."

I had barely put on my coat when I got another call: "Jaggi's been arrested. Well, not exactly arrested. More like kidnapped." My first thought was that it was my fault: I had asked Jaggi Singh to tell me his whereabouts over a cellphone: our call must have been monitored—that's how they found him. If that sounds paranoid, welcome to Summit City.

Less than an hour later, at the Comité Populaire St-Jean Baptiste community centre, a group of six swollen-eyed witnesses read me their handwritten accounts of how the most visible organizer of yesterday's direct-action protest against the Free Trade Area of the Americas was snatched from under their noses. All say that Singh was standing around talking to friends, urging them to move farther away from the breached security fence. They all say he was trying to de-escalate the police standoff.

"He said it was getting too tense," said Mike Stauden-maier, a U.S. activist who was talking to Singh when he was grabbed from behind, then surrounded by three large men.

"They were dressed like activists," said Helen Nazon, a twenty-three-year-old from Quebec City, "with hooded sweatshirts, bandanas on their faces, flannel shirts, a little grubby. They pushed Jaggi on the ground and kicked him. It was really violent."

"Then they dragged him off," said Michèle Luellen. All the witnesses told me that when Singh's friends closed in to try to rescue him, the men dressed as activists pulled out long batons, beat back the crowd and identified themselves: "Police!" they shouted. Then they threw him into a beige van and drove off. Several of the young activists have open cuts where they were hit.

Three hours after Singh's arrest, there was still no word of where he was being held.

Nabbing activists off the streets and throwing them into unmarked cars is not supposed to happen in Canada. But in Jaggi Singh's short career as a globalization activist, it has happened to him before—during the 1997 protests against the Asia Pacific Economic Cooperation summit. The day before the protests took place, he was grabbed by two plain-clothes police officers while walking alone on the University of British Columbia campus, thrown to the ground, then stuffed into an unmarked car.

The charge, he later found out, was assault. He had

apparently talked so loudly into a megaphone some weeks before that it had hurt the eardrum of a nearby police officer. The charge, of course, was later dropped, but the point was clearly to have him behind bars during the protest, just as he will no doubt be in custody for today's march. He faced a similar arrest in October at the Group of 20 summit for finance ministers in Montreal. In all these bizarre cases, Jaggi Singh has never been convicted of vandalism, of planning or plotting violent activity. Anyone who has seen him in action knows that his greatest crime is giving good speeches.

That's why I was on the phone with him minutes before his arrest—trying to persuade him to come to the Peoples' Summit teach-in that I was co-hosting to tell the crowd of fifteen hundred what was going on in the streets. He had agreed but then determined it was too difficult to cross the city.

I can't help thinking the reason that this young man has been treated as a terrorist, repeatedly and with no evidence, might have something to do with his brown skin and the fact that his last name is Singh. No wonder his friends say that this supposed threat to the state doesn't like to walk alone at night.

After collecting all the witness statements, the small crowd begins to leave the community centre to attend a late-night planning meeting. There is a commotion in the doorway, and in an instant the halls are filled with red-faced people, their eyes streaming with tears, frantically looking for running water.

The tear gas has filled the street outside the centre and

has entered the corridors. "This is no longer a Green Zone! *Les flics* [the police] *s'en viennent!*" So much for making it to my laptop at the hotel.

Denis Belanger, who was kind enough to let me use the community centre's rickety PC to write this column, notices that the message light is flashing on the phone. It turns out that the police have closed in the entire area—no one is getting out.

"Maybe I'll spend the night," Belanger said. Maybe I will too.

Indiscriminate Tear-Gassing
Toxic fumes bring disparate groups together during the FTAA protests

April 2001

The protests are over, the scapegoating has begun. Maude Barlow, chair of the Council of Canadians, is condemned for not calling off "Maude's Mob." Activist Jaggi Singh is in jail for allegedly possessing a weapon that he never owned or used—a theatrical catapult that shot stuffed animals over the infamous fence in Quebec City during last weekend's Summit of the Americas.

It's not just that the police didn't get the joke, it's that they don't get the new era of political protest, one adapted to our postmodern times. There was no one person, or group, who could call off "their people," because the tens of thousands who came out to protest against the Free Trade Area of the Americas are part of a movement that doesn't have a leader, a centre or even an agreed-on name. Yet it exists, undeniably, nonetheless.

What is difficult to convey in media reports is that there weren't two protests that took place in Quebec City—one a "peaceful" labour march, the other a "violent" anarchist riot—there were hundreds of protests. One was organized by a mother and daughter from Montreal. Another by a van-load of grad students from Edmonton. Another by three friends from Toronto who aren't members of anything but their health clubs. Yet another by a couple of waiters from a local café on their lunch break.

Sure, there were well-organized groups in Quebec City: the unions had buses, matching placards and a parade route; the Black Bloc of anarchists had gas masks and radio links. But for days, the streets were also filled with people who simply said to a friend, "Let's go to Quebec," and with Quebec City residents who said, "Let's go outside." They didn't join one big protest, they participated in a moment.

How could it be otherwise? The traditional institutions that once organized citizens into neat, structured groups are all in decline: unions, religions, political parties. Yet something propelled tens of thousands of individuals to the streets anyway, an intuition, a gut instinct—perhaps just the profoundly human desire to be part of something larger than oneself.

Did they have their party line together, a detailed dissection of the ins and outs of the FTAA? Not always. But neither can the Quebec protests be dismissed as vacuous political tourism. George W. Bush's message at the summit was that the mere acts of buying and selling would do our governing for us. "Trade helps spread freedom," he said.

It was precisely this impoverished and passive vision of democracy that was being rejected on the streets outside. Whatever else the protesters were seeking, all were certainly looking for a taste of direct political participation. The result of these hundreds of miniature protests converging was chaotic, sometimes awful, but frequently inspiring. One thing is certain: after finally shaking off the mantle of political spectatorship, these people are not about to hand over the reins to a cabal of would-be leaders.

The protesters will become more organized, however, a fact that has more to do with the actions of the police than the directives of Maude Barlow, Jaggi Singh or, for that matter, me. If people wandered and stumbled to Quebec City, profoundly unsure of what it meant to be part of a political movement, something united us once we arrived: mass arrests, rubber bullets and, most of all, a thick white blanket of gas.

Despite the government line of praising "good" protesters while condemning "bad" ones, treatment of everyone on the streets of Quebec City was crude, cowardly and indiscriminate. The security forces used the actions of a few rock throwers as a camera-friendly justification to do what they had been trying to do from the start: clear the city of thousands of lawful protesters because it was more convenient that way.

Once they got their "provocation," they filled entire neighbourhoods with tear gas, a substance that by definition does not discriminate, is indifferent to perimeters, protest tactics or politics. The toxic fumes seeped into houses, forcing families to breathe through masks in their living rooms. Frustrated that the wind was against them, the police sprayed some more. People giving the peace sign to the police were gassed. People handing out food were gassed. I met a fifty-year-old woman from Ottawa who told me cheerfully, "I went out to buy a sandwich and was gassed twice." People having a party under a bridge were gassed. People protesting against their friends' arrests were gassed. The first-aid clinic treating people who had been gassed was gassed.

Tear gas was supposed to break down the protesters, but it had the opposite effect: it enraged and radicalized them, enough to cheer for members of the Black Bloc anarchist contingent who dared to throw back the canisters. Gas may be light and atomized enough to ride on air, but I suspect the coming months will show that it also has powerful bonding properties.

[*The Ligue des Droits (Human Rights League) of Quebec eventually issued a report about police violence at the summit. The report documented several incidents that had not been reported, including that police used a laser-guided scope to fire a plastic bullet into the genitals of one protester. A man already lying on the ground was shocked with a police stun gun, and a stilt-walker dressed as the Statue of Liberty was taken out at the knees by a water cannon as she approached the fence. The same report detailed appalling mistreatment of those arrested. Some protesters were kept handcuffed in police buses for eight hours in heavily gassed areas before being taken to jail. Once there, many were strip-searched and hosed down with cold water ("decontamination" for the gas). And despite the fact that authorities cleared the local prison before the protests (at a cost of $5 million), many of the arrested were held four or five to a single-person cell.*]

Getting Used to Violence
How years of police brutality culminated in the death of Italian protester Carlo Giuliani

August 2001

On July 20, 2001, at the G8 meeting in Genoa, the Italian police shot a twenty-three-year-old protester, Carlo Giuliani, at close range in the head and backed over his body in a jeep. This is an excerpt from a speech given in Reggio Emilia, Italy, one month later at the Festival dell'Unità.

I have been covering this wave of protest for five years. And I have watched with horror as the police have moved from pepper spray to mass tear gas; from tear gas to rubber bullets; rubber bullets to live ammunition. Just this summer, we have seen an escalation from severe injuries of protesters in Gothenburg, Sweden, to, in Genoa, a protester shot dead, then backed over by a police jeep. Nearby, activists sleeping in a school were woken and beaten bloody, their teeth scattered on the ground.

How did this happen so quickly? I have to conclude, with much regret, that it happened because we let it happen, and by "we" I mean all the good left liberals in media, academia and the arts who tell themselves they believe in civil liberties. In Canada, when we first started seeing police pepper-spray and strip-search young activists a few years ago, there was a public outcry. It was front-page news. We asked questions and demanded answers, accountability from the police. People said, those are our kids, idealists, future leaders. But you rarely hear those sorts of sentiments expressed in the face of police violence against protesters these days. The lack of investigation by journalists, the lack of outrage from left parties, from academics, from NGOs that exist to protect freedom of expression, has been scandalous.

Young activists have faced enormous public scrutiny for their actions; their motivations and their tactics have all been questioned. If the police had faced one-tenth of the scrutiny that this movement has, maybe the brutality that we saw last month in Genoa wouldn't have happened. I say this because the last time I was in Italy was in June, more than a month before the protests. At that time, it was already clear that the police were running out of control, getting their excuses ready for a major civil liberties crackdown and setting the stage for extreme violence. Before a single activist had taken to the streets, a pre-emptive state of emergency had been essentially declared: airports were closed and much of the city was cordoned off. Yet when I was last in Italy, all the public discussions focused not on these violations of civil liberties but on the alleged threat posed by activists.

Police brutality feeds off public indifference, slipping into social crevices that we have long ignored. *Newsweek* described Carlo Giuliani's death as the movement's "first blood." But that conveniently erases the blood that is so often spilled when protests against corporate power take place in poor countries, or impoverished parts of rich countries, when those resisting are not white.

Two weeks before the G8 came to Genoa, three students were killed in Papua New Guinea protesting a World Bank privatization scheme. It barely made the news, yet it was the very same issue that has brought thousands to the streets during so-called anti-globalization protests.

It is not a coincidence that police violence always thrives in marginalized communities, whether the guns are pointed at Zapatista communities in Chiapas, Mexico, or at indigenous communities in peaceful Canada, when First Nations activists decide to use direct action to defend their land.

The police take their cue from us: when we walk away, they walk in. The real ammunition is not rubber bullets and tear gas. It is our silence.

Manufacturing Threats
The Italian government cracks down on civil liberties after Genoa

September 5, 2001

Part of the tourist ritual of traipsing through Italy in August is marvelling at how the locals have mastered the art of living—and then complaining bitterly about how everything is closed.

"So civilized," you hear North Americans remarking over four-course lunches. "Now somebody open up that store and sell me some Pradas!" This year, August in Italy was a little different. Many of the southern beach towns where Italians hide from tourists were half-empty, and the cities never paused. When I arrived two weeks ago, journalists, politicians and activists all reported that it was the first summer of their lives when they didn't take a single day off.

How could they? First there was Genoa, then After Genoa.

The fallout from protests against the G8 in July is redrawing the country's political landscape—and everybody wants a chance to shape the results. Newspapers are breaking circulation records. Meetings—anything having to do with politics—are bursting at the seams. In Naples, I went to an activist planning session about an upcoming NATO summit; more than seven hundred people crammed into a sweltering classroom to argue about "the movement's strategy

After Genoa." Two days later, near Bologna, a conference about politics After Genoa drew two thousand; they stayed until 11 P.M.

The stakes in this period are high. Were the 200,000 (some say 300,000) people on the streets an unstoppable force that will eventually unseat Prime Minister Silvio Berlusconi? Or will Genoa be the beginning of a long silence, a time when citizens equate mass gatherings with terrifying violence?

In the first weeks after the summit, attention was focused squarely on the brutality of the Italian police: the killing of young Carlo Giuliani, reports of torture in the prisons, the bloody midnight raid on the school where activists slept.

But Berlusconi, whose training is in advertising, is not about to relinquish the meaning of Genoa that easily. In recent weeks, he has been furiously recasting himself as "a good father," determined to save his family from imminent danger. Lacking a real threat, he has manufactured one—an obscure United Nations conference on hunger, scheduled for Rome from November 5 to November 9, 2001. To much media fanfare, Berlusconi has announced that the Food and Agriculture Organization (FAO) meeting will not be held in "sacred Rome" because "I don't want to see our cities smashed and burnt." Instead, it will be held somewhere remote (much like Canada's plans to hold the next G8 meeting in secluded Kananaskis, Alberta).

This is shadow boxing at its best. No one had planned to disrupt the FAO meeting. The event would have attracted some minor protest, mostly from critics of genetically modified crops. Some hoped the meeting would be an opportunity to debate the root causes of hunger, just like the UN Conference on Racism in Durban, South Africa, has stepped up the debate about slavery reparations.

Jacques Diouf, director of FAO, seems to be relishing the unexpected attention. After all, despite being saddled with the crushing mandate of cutting world hunger in half, the FAO attracts almost no outside interest—from politicians or protesters. The organization's biggest problem is that it is so uncontroversial it's practically invisible.

"For all these arguments about change of venue, I would like to say I am very grateful," Diouf told reporters last week. "Now people in every country know that there will be a summit to talk about the problems of hunger." [*In the end, the meeting was delayed until June 2002. It took place in Rome without incident.*]

But even though the threat of anti-FAO violence was dreamed up by Berlusconi, his actions are part of a serious assault on civil liberties in After-Genoa Italy. On Sunday, Italy's Parliamentary Relations Minister Carlo Giovanardi said that during November's FAO meeting, "demonstrations in the capital will be prohibited. It is a duty," he said, "to ban demonstrations in certain places and at certain times." There may be a similar ban on public assembly in Naples during the upcoming NATO ministers' meeting, which has also been moved to a military compound on the outskirts of the city.

There was even talk of cancelling a concert by Manu Chao in Naples last Friday. The musician supports the Zapatistas, sings about "illegal" immigrants, and he played to the crowds in Genoa. That, apparently, was enough for the police to smell a riot in the making. In a country that remembers the logic of authoritarianism, this is all chillingly familiar: first create a climate of fear and tension, then suspend constitutional rights in the interest of protecting "public order."

So far, Italians seem unwilling to play into Berlusconi's hand. The Manu Chao concert took place as planned. There was, of course, no violence. But seventy thousand people did dance like crazy in the pouring rain, a much needed release after a long and difficult summer.

The crowds of police ringing the concert looked on. They seemed tired, as if they could have used a day off.

Stuck in the Spectacle
Is this becoming a McMovement?

May 2001

The idea of turning London into a life-size Monopoly board on May Day sounded like a great idea.

Despite familiar criticism lobbed at modern protesters that they lack focus and clear goals such as "Save the trees" or "Drop the debt," the current wave of anti-corporate activism is itself a response to the limitations of single-issue politics. Tired of treating the symptoms of an economic model—underfunded hospitals, homelessness, widening disparity, exploding prisons, climate change—campaigners are now making a clear attempt to "out" the system behind the symptoms. But how do you hold a protest against abstract economic ideas without sounding hideously strident or all over the map?

How about using the board game that has taught generations of kids about land ownership? The organizers of yesterday's May Day Monopoly protest issued annotated maps of London featuring such familiar sites as Regent Street, Pall Mall and Trafalgar Square, encouraging participants to situate their May Day actions on the Monopoly board. Want to protest against privatization? Go to a rail station. Industrial agriculture? McDonald's at King's Cross. Fossil fuels? The electric company. And always carry your "Get out of jail free" card.

The problem was that by yesterday afternoon London didn't look like an ingenious mix of popular education and street theatre. It looked pretty much like every other mass protest these days: demonstrators penned in by riot police, smashed windows, boarded-up shops, running fights with police. And in the pre-protest media wars, there was more déjà vu. Were protesters planning violence? Would the presence of six thousand police officers itself provoke violence? Why won't all the protesters condemn violence? Why does everybody always talk about violence?

This, it seems, is what protests look like today. Let's call it McProtest, because it's becoming the same all over. And of course I've written about all this before. In fact, almost all my recent writing has been about the right to assembly, security fences, tear gas and dodgy arrests. Or else it has tried to dispel wilful misrepresentations of the protesters—for instance, that they are "anti-trade," or long for a pre-agrarian utopia.

It is an article of faith in most activist circles that mass demonstrations are always positive: they build morale, display strength, attract media attention. But what seems to be getting lost is that demonstrations themselves aren't a movement. They are only the flashy displays of everyday movements, grounded in schools, workplaces and neighbourhoods. Or at least they should be.

I keep thinking about the historic day, on March 11 this year, when the Zapatista commanders entered Mexico City—an army that led a successful uprising against the state, yet the residents of Mexico City didn't quake in fear—200,000 of them came out to greet the Zapatistas. Streets were closed to traffic, but no one seemed concerned about the inconvenience to commuters. And shopkeepers didn't board up their windows; they held "revolution" sidewalk sales.

Is this because the Zapatistas are less dangerous than a few urban anarchists in white overalls? Hardly. It was because the march on Mexico City was seven years in the making (some would say five hundred years, but that's another story). Years of building coalitions with other indigenous groups, with workers in the *maquiladora* factories, with students, with intellectuals and journalists; years of mass consultations, of open *encuentros* (meetings) of six thousand people. The event in Mexico City wasn't the movement; it was only a very public demonstration of all that invisible daily work.

The most powerful resistance movements are always deeply rooted in community—and are accountable to those communities. But one of the greatest challenges of living in the high consumer culture that was being protested in London yesterday is the reality of rootlessness. Few of us know our neighbours, talk about much more at work than shopping, or have time for community politics. How can a movement be accountable when communities are fraying?

Within a context of urban rootlessness, there are clearly moments to demonstrate, but perhaps more important, there are moments to build the connections that make demonstration something more than theatre. There are times when radicalism means standing up to the police, but there are many more times when it means talking to your neighbour.

The issues behind yesterday's May Day demonstrations are no longer marginal. Food scares, genetic engineering, climate change, income inequality, failed privatization schemes—these are all front-page news. Yet something is gravely wrong when the protests still seem deracinated, cut off from urgent daily concerns. It means that the spectacle of displaying a movement is getting confused with the less glamorous business of building one.

CAPITALIZING ON TERROR

In which September 11 is used to silence critics, ram
through new trade deals, "re-brand" the U.S.A.—
and turn bra shopping into a patriotic duty

IV

CAPITALIZING ON TERROR

In which September 11 is used to silence critics, push
through new trade deals, "re-brand" the U.S.A.
and turn bio shopping into a patriotic duty

The Brutal Calculus of Suffering
When some lives seem to count more than others

October 2001

This speech was delivered at the Mediemötet 2001 conference in Stockholm, Sweden. The "Media Meeting" was a three-day gathering of journalists celebrating the hundredth anniversary of the Swedish Federation of Journalism.

It's a true privilege to be able to address so many of Sweden's leading journalists at this important juncture for our profession. When I was invited to this conference six months ago, I was asked to talk about globalization and corporate concentration in the media, as well as the issues at the heart of the global protest movements: widening inequality and international double standards. I'm still going to touch on these themes, but I'm also going to discuss how they relate to the events that I know are on all our minds today: last month's attacks on the U.S. and the ongoing U.S.-led bombing campaign in Afghanistan.

To this end, let me begin with a story. When I was twenty-three, I had my first media job as a copy editor at a newspaper. The newspaper closed at 11 P.M., but two people stayed until 1 A.M. in case a news story broke that was so significant it was worth reopening the front page. On the first night that it was my turn to stay late, a tornado in a southern U.S. state killed three people, and the senior editor on duty decided to reopen the front page. On my second night, I read on the wires that 114 people had just been killed in Afghanistan, so I dutifully flagged down the senior editor. Remember, I was young, and it seemed to me that if three people warranted reopening the front page, then 114 people would surely classify as a major news event. I will never forget what that editor told me. "Don't worry," he said, "those people kill each other all the time."

Since September 11, I've been thinking again about that incident, about how we in the media participate in a process that confirms and reconfirms the idea that death and murder are tragic, extraordinary and intolerable in some places and banal, ordinary, unavoidable, even expected in others.

Because, frankly, I still have some of that naive twenty-three-year-old in me. And I still think the idea that some blood is precious, some blood is cheap is not just morally wrong but has helped to bring us to this bloody moment in our history.

That cold, brutal, almost unconscious calculus works its way into our shared global psyche and twists and maims us. It breeds the recklessness of those who know they are invisible, that they are not among the counted. Are we, in the media, neutral observers of this deadly mathematics?

No. Sadly, it is we who do much of the counting. It is we who have the power to choose whose lives are presented in Technicolor, and whose in shades of grey. It is we who decide when to cry "tragedy" and when to shrug "ordinary"; when to celebrate heroes and when to let the bloodless statistics tell the story; who gets to be an anonymous victim—like the Africans killed in the U.S. embassy bombings in 1998—and who gets to have a story, a family, a life—like the firefighters in New York.

On September 11, watching TV replays of the buildings exploding over and over again in New York and Washington, I couldn't help thinking about all the times media coverage has protected us from similar horrors elsewhere. During the Gulf War, for instance, we didn't see real buildings exploding or people fleeing, we saw a sterile Space Invader battlefield, a bomb's-eye view of concrete targets—there and then gone. Who was in those abstract polygons? We never found out.

Americans still don't get regular coverage on CNN of the ongoing bombings in Iraq, nor are they treated to human interest stories on the devastating effects of economic sanctions on that country's children. After the 1998 bombing of a pharmaceutical factory in Sudan (mistaken for a chemical weapons facility), there weren't too many follow-up reports about what the loss of vaccine manufacturing did to disease prevention in the region.

And when NATO bombed civilian targets in Kosovo—including markets, hospitals, refugee convoys, passenger trains—NBC didn't do "streeter" interviews with survivors about how shocked they were by the indiscriminate destruction.

What has come to be called "video-game war coverage" is merely a reflection of the idea that has guided American foreign policy since the Gulf War: that it's possible to intervene in conflicts around the world—in Iraq, Kosovo,

Afghanistan—while suffering only minimal U.S. casualties. The United States government has come to believe in the ultimate oxymoron: a safe war.

And it is this logic, mirrored repeatedly in our lopsided coverage of global conflicts, that is helping to feed a blinding rage in many parts of the world, a rage at the persistent asymmetry of suffering. This is the context in which twisted revenge seekers come less with a set of concrete demands than a visceral need for U.S. citizens to share their pain.

It's easy for those of us in the media to tell ourselves that we have no choice but to participate in this brutal calculus. Of course we care more about the loss of some people than others. The world is simply too filled with bloodshed to grieve each death, even each mass slaughter. So we make arbitrary distinctions just to get through the day: we care about children more than adults; we care about people who look like us more than those who don't.

This is, perhaps, natural, if one dares use such a word. But these calculations become much more troubling in the context of rapidly consolidated global media empires, which are now the primary news sources for so many people around the world. CNN, BBC and NewsCorp—though they may try to appear international, even placeless—still report from clearly American and European perspectives. When they say "we," it is a we filtered through Atlanta, London or New York. The question is, What happens when the narrow cultural assumptions of that "we," that "us," are beamed out to the farthest corners of our deeply divided world, badly disguised as a global "we"?

This process of universalization is rarely questioned, especially by those who produce global media. It's assumed that we share a culture now: we watch the same bad movies, we all love Jennifer Lopez, we wear Nikes and eat McDonald's, so naturally we should mourn the same deaths: of Diana or the New York firefighters. But the transmission is inevitably one-way. The global "we"—as defined by London and New York—now reaches into places that are clearly not included in its narrow perimeters, into homes and bars where local losses are not treated as global losses, where those local losses are somehow diminished relative to the grandness, the globalness of our own projected pain.

As journalists perhaps we would rather not face the effects of our calculations but we can no longer avoid them. Our parochial biases, thanks to global satellites, are there for all to see, and as we globalize our own suffering, "they" get the message that they are not "us"—not part of the global "we." And they become very, very angry.

Since September 11, I have spoken with friends from South Africa and Iran who are furious about the outpouring of grief demanded of them in response to the attacks. They say it is racist to ask the world to mourn and avenge U.S. deaths when so many deaths in their countries go unmourned, unavenged. I have argued with these friends that this is a moral dead end, that mourning each other's terrible losses is surely what it means to be human. And yet, I've come to accept, with much reluctance, that perhaps I am asking too much. Perhaps from those who have seen so much indifference to the loss of their own loved ones, so much asymmetry of compassion, we in the West have, at least temporarily, forfeited the right to expect compassion in return.

In Canada, we have just gone through a high-profile scandal because one of the country's leading feminists referred to America's foreign policy as "soaked in blood." Unacceptable, many said, in the wake of the attacks on the U.S. Some even wanted to charge her with hate speech. Defending herself against her critics, Sunera Thobani, once an immigrant to Canada, said she chose her words carefully, in order to make the point that despite the disembodied language of smart bombs, precision weapons and collateral damage, victims of U.S. aggression also bleed.

"It is an attempt to humanize these peoples in profoundly graphic terms," she writes. "It compels us to recognize the sheer corporeality of the terrain upon which bombs rain and mass terror is waged. This language calls on 'us' to recognize that 'they' bleed just like 'we' do, that 'they' hurt and suffer just like 'us.'"

This, it seems, is the "civilization" we are fighting for: battles over who is allowed to bleed. "Compassion," a friend wrote to me last week, "is not a zero sum game. But there is also undeniably something unbearable in the hierarchy of death (1 American equals 2 west Europeans equals 10 Yugoslavs equals 50 Arabs equals 200 Africans), which is one part power, one part wealth, one part race."

As media makers we need to look deeply into our own work, and ask ourselves what we are doing to feed this devaluation of human lives and the rage and recklessness that flow from it. Traditionally, we are far too used to patting ourselves on the back, convinced that our work makes people more compassionate, more connected. Remember that satellite television was supposed to bring democracy to the world—or so we were told in 1989. Viacom International chairman Sumner Redstone once said, "We put MTV into East Germany, and the next day the Berlin Wall fell," while Rupert Murdoch said that "satellite broadcasting makes it possible for information-hungry residents of many closed societies to bypass state-controlled television."

And yet a decade later, it's now clear that instead of bringing democracy, global TV has flaunted inequalities and asymmetries and sparked waves of resentment. In 1989, Western journalists were seen as allies of liberation struggles. "The whole world is watching," crowds chanted during the Velvet Revolution and in Tiananmen Square. Now, journalists are used to being shouted down by protesters who see them as part of a system that persistently glosses over inequalities and marginalizes dissenting voices. And this week, tragically, some U.S. journalists are opening letters filled with white powder, suddenly, bewilderingly, subjects in the story they are supposed to be covering.

So much of this conflict is about who and what gets seen and heard, whose lives are counted. The attacks in New York and Washington were clearly designed not just as strikes but also as spectacle, for their theatrical charge. And they were captured from every camera angle, played and replayed, lived and relived. But what about what is going on in Afghanistan right now? The U.S. State Department has asked TV networks and newspapers not to run bin Laden's communications because they might arouse anti-American sentiment. And for $2 million a month, the Pentagon has purchased exclusive rights to the entire capacity of the only private satellite over Afghanistan that provides high enough resolution that you can see human beings.

If we could see the images on our television screens—human casualties, refugees fleeing—it might mean that the death and destruction in Afghanistan would begin, in some small way, to take on the same sort of reality and humanity as the deaths in New York and Washington. We would have to confront actual people instead of looking at a sterile video game. But none of the images can be released without Defense Department approval—ever.

This silent war over whose lives are counted, whose deaths are collectively mourned, long predates September 11. Indeed, much of the shock of September 11 had to do with how much global suffering was all but invisible in the mainstream U.S. press, pushed aside by the euphoria of prosperity and trade.

And so, on September 11, America woke up in the middle of a war only to find out that the war had been going on for years—but no one told them. They were hearing about OJ instead of the devastating effects of economic sanctions on Iraqi children. They were hearing about Monica instead of the fallout from the bombing of that pharmaceutical factory. They were learning about *Survivor* instead of the role the CIA had played in financing the Mujahedeen warriors. "Here's the rub," writes the Indian novelist,

Arundhati Roy, "America is at war against people it doesn't know, because they don't appear much on TV."

Christopher Isherwood once wrote about Americans that "the Europeans hate us because we've retired to live inside our advertisements, like hermits going into caves to contemplate." This retreat into a self-referential media cocoon goes some way toward explaining why the attacks of September 11 seemed to come not from another country but from another planet—a parallel universe, such was the disorientation and dislocation.

But instead of backing up and filling this gap—of information, of analysis, of understanding—we hear instead a chorus: this came out of nowhere, it is inexplicable, it has no past; "they" hate us; they want to take away our democracies, our liberties, our stuff. Instead of asking why the attacks happened, our television networks simply play them over again.

Just when Americans most need information about the outside world—and their country's complicated and troubling place in it—they are only getting themselves reflected back, over and over and over: Americans weeping, Americans recovering, Americans cheering, Americans praying. A media house of mirrors, when what we all need are more windows on the world.

New Opportunists
Trade negotiations are now infused with the righteousness of a holy war

October 2001

There are many contenders for Biggest Political Opportunist since the September 11 atrocities: politicians ramming through life-changing laws while voters are still mourning, corporations diving for public cash, pundits accusing their opponents of treason. Yet amid the chorus of draconian proposals and McCarthyite threats, one voice of opportunism still stands out. That voice belongs to Robyn Mazer. She is using September 11 to call for an international crackdown on counterfeit T-shirts.

Not surprisingly, Mazer is a trade lawyer in Washington. Even less surprising, she specializes in trade laws that protect the United States' single largest export: copyright. That's music, movies, logos, seed patents, software and much more. TRIPS (trade-related intellectual property rights) is one of the most controversial side agreements in the run-up to the November 2001 World Trade Organization meeting in Qatar. It is the battleground for disputes ranging from Brazil's right to disseminate generic AIDS drugs to China's thriving market in knock-off Britney Spears CDs.

American multinationals are desperate to gain access to these large markets, but they want protection. Many poor countries, meanwhile, say TRIPS costs millions to police, while strangleholds on intellectual property drive up costs for local industries and consumers.

What does any of this trade wrangling have to do with terrorism? Nothing, absolutely nothing. Unless, of course, you ask Robyn Mazer, who wrote an article last week in *The Washington Post* headlined, "From T-shirts to terrorism; that fake Nike swoosh may be helping fund bin Laden's network."

She writes, "Recent developments suggest that many of the governments suspected of supporting al-Qaeda are also promoting, being corrupted by, or at the very least ignoring highly lucrative trafficking in counterfeit and pirated products capable of generating huge money flows to terrorists."

"Suggest," "suspected of," "at the very least," "capable of"—that's a lot of hedging for one sentence, especially from someone who used to work in the U.S. Department of Justice. But the conclusion is unambiguous: you either enforce TRIPS or you are with the terrorists. Welcome to the brave new world of trade negotiations, where every arcane clause is infused with the righteousness of a holy war.

Robyn Mazer's political opportunism raises some interesting contradictions. U.S. Trade Representative Robert Zoellick has been using September 11 for another opportunistic goal: to secure "fast track" trade-negotiating power for President George W. Bush, which would give him free rein to negotiate new trade deals that Congress could either accept or reject but not amend. According to Zoellick, these new powers are needed because trade "promotes the values at the heart of this protracted struggle."

What do new trade deals have to do with fighting terrorism? Well, the terrorists, we are told, hate America precisely because they hate consumerism: McDonald's and Nike and capitalism—you know, freedom. To trade is therefore to defy their ascetic crusade, to spread the very products they loathe.

But wait a minute: what about all those fakes Mazer says are bankrolling terror? In Afghanistan, she claims, you can buy "T-shirts bearing counterfeit Nike logos and glorifying bin Laden as 'The great mujahid of Islam.'" It seems we are facing a much more complicated scenario than the facile dichotomy of a consumerist McWorld versus an anti-consumer jihad. If Mazer is correct, not only are the two worlds thoroughly enmeshed, the imagery of McWorld is being used to finance jihad.

Maybe a little complexity isn't so bad. Part of the disorientation many Americans now face has to do with the inflated and oversimplified place that consumerism plays in the American narrative. To buy is to be. To buy is to love. To buy is to vote. People outside the U.S. who want Nikes—even counterfeit Nikes—must want to be American, must love America, must in some way be voting for everything America stands for.

This has been the fairy tale since 1989, when the same media companies that are bringing us America's "war on terrorism" proclaimed that their television satellites would topple dictatorships the world over. Consumption would lead to freedom. But all these easy narratives are breaking down: authoritarianism co-exists with consumerism, desire for American products is mixed with rage at inequality.

Nothing exposes these contradictions more clearly than the trade wars raging over "fake" goods. Pirating thrives in the deep craters of global inequality, when demand for consumer goods is decades ahead of purchasing power. It thrives in China, where goods made in export-only sweatshops are sold for more than factory workers make in a month. In Africa, where the price of AIDS drugs is a cruel joke. In Brazil, where CD pirates are feted as musical Robin Hoods.

Complexity is lousy for opportunism. But it does help us get closer to the truth, even if it means sorting through a lot of fakes.

Kamikaze Capitalists
During the WTO talks in Qatar, trade negotiators were the true believers

November 2001

What do you call someone who believes so firmly in the promise of salvation through a set of rigid rules that he is willing to risk his own life to spread those rules? A religious fanatic? A holy warrior? How about a U.S. trade negotiator?

On Friday, the World Trade Organization begins its meeting in Doha, Qatar. According to U.S. security briefings, there is reason to believe that al-Qaeda, which has plenty of fans in the Persian Gulf state, has managed to get some of its operatives into the country, including an explosives specialist. Some terrorists may even have infiltrated the Qatari military. Given these threats, you might think that the United States and the WTO would have cancelled the meeting. But not these true believers.

Instead, U.S. delegates have been kitted out with gas masks, two-way radios and drugs to combat bioterrorism. (Canadian delegates have been issued the drugs as well.) As negotiators wrangle over agricultural subsidies, softwood lumber and pharmaceutical patents, helicopters will be waiting to whisk U.S. delegates onto aircraft carriers parked in the Persian Gulf, ready for a Batman-style getaway. It's safe to say that Doha isn't your average trade negotiation; it's something new. Call it Kamikaze Capitalism.

Last week, U.S. Trade Representative Robert Zoellick praised his delegation for being willing to "sacrifice" in the face of such "undoubted risks." Why are they doing it? Probably for the same reason people have always put their lives on the line for a cause: they believe in a set of rules that promises transcendence.

In this case, the god is economic growth, and it promises to save us from global recession. New markets to access, new sectors to privatize, new regulations to slash—these will get those arrows in the corner of our television screens pointing heavenward once again.

Of course, growth cannot be created at a meeting, but Doha can accomplish something else, something more religious than economic. It can send "a sign" to the market, a sign that growth is on the way, that expansion is just around the corner. And an ambitious new round of WTO negotiations is the sign they are praying for. For rich countries like ours, the desire for this sign is desperate. It is more pressing than any possible problems with current WTO rules, problems mostly raised by poor countries fed up with a system that has pushed them to drop their trade barriers while rich countries kept theirs up.

So it's no surprise that poor countries are this round's strongest opponents. Before they agree to drastically expand the WTO's reach, many are asking rich countries to make good on their promises from the last round. There are major disputes swirling around agricultural subsidies and dumping, about tariffs on garments and the patenting of life forms. The most contentious issue is drug patents. India, Brazil, Thailand and a coalition of African countries want clear language stating that patents can be overridden to protect public health. The U.S. and Canada are not just resisting—they are resisting even as their own delegates head for Qatar popping discount Cipros, muscled out of Bayer using exactly the kind of pressure tactics they are calling unfair trade practices.

These concerns are not reflected in the draft ministerial declaration. Which is why Nigeria just blasted the WTO for being "one-sided" and "disregarding the concerns of the developing and least developed countries." India's WTO ambassador said last week that the draft "gives the uncomfortable impression that there is no serious attempt to bring issues of importance to developing countries into the mainstream."

These protests have made little impression with the WTO. Growth is the only god at the negotiations, and any measures that could slow profits even slightly—of drug companies, of water companies, of oil companies—are being treated by believers as if they are on the side of the infidels and evildoers.

What we are witnessing is trade being "bundled" (Microsoft-style) inside the with-us-or-against logic of the "war on terrorism". Last week, Zoellick explained that "by promoting the WTO's agenda . . . these 142 nations can counter the revulsive destructionism of terrorism." Open markets, he said, are "an antidote" to the terrorists' "violent rejectionism." (Fittingly, these are non-arguments glued together with made-up words.)

He further called on WTO member states to set aside their petty concerns about mass hunger and AIDS and join the economic front of America's war. "We hope the representatives who meet in Doha will perceive the larger stakes," he said.

Trade negotiations are all about power and opportunity, and for Doha's Kamikaze Capitalists, terrorism is just another opportunity to leverage. Perhaps their motto can be Nietzsche's maxim: What doesn't kill us will make us stronger. Much stronger.

The Terrifying Return of Great Men
When a few people decide to live larger than life, we all get trampled

December 2001

Since the release of the Video, Osama bin Laden's every gesture, chuckle and word has been dissected. But with all the attention on bin Laden, his co-star in the video, identified in the official transcript only as "Sheik," has received little scrutiny. Too bad, since no matter who he is (and there are several theories), he offers a rare window into the psychology of men who think of mass murder as a great game.

A theme that comes up repeatedly in the giddy monologues of bin Laden's guest is the idea that they are living in times as grand as those described in the Koran. This war, he observes, is like "in the days of the Prophet Muhammad. Exactly like what's happening right now." He goes on to say that "it will be similar to the early days of Al-Mujahedeen and Al-Ansar [similar to the early days of Islam]." And just in case we didn't get the picture: "Like the old days, such as Abu Bakr and Uthman and Ali and others. In these days, in our times . . ."

It's easy to chalk up this nostalgia to the usual theory about Osama bin Laden's followers being stuck in the Middle Ages. But the comments seem to reflect something more. It's not some ascetic medieval lifestyle that he longs for, but the idea of living in mythic times, when men were godlike, battles were epic and history was spelled with a capital H. Screw you, Francis Fukuyama, he seems to be saying. History hasn't ended yet. We are making it, right here, right now!

It's an idea we've heard from many quarters since September 11, a return of the great narrative: chosen men, evil empires, master plans and great battles. All are ferociously back in style. The Bible, the Koran, the Clash of Civilizations, *The Lord of the Rings*—all of them suddenly playing out "in these days, in our times."

This redemption narrative is our most persistent myth, and it has a dangerous flip side. When a few men decide to live their myths, to be larger than life, it can't help having an impact on all those whose lives unfold in regular sizes. People suddenly look insignificant by comparison, easy to sacrifice in the name of some greater purpose.

When the Berlin Wall fell, it was supposed to have buried this epic narrative in its rubble. That was capitalism's decisive victory.

Francis Fukuyama's end-of-history theory was understandably infuriating to those who lost that gladiatorial battle, whether they favoured a triumph for global communism or, in Osama bin Laden's case, an imperialist version of Islam. What is clear post–September 11, however, is that history's end also turned out to be a hollow victory for America's own Cold Warriors. It seems that since 1989, many of them have missed their epic narrative as if it were a lost limb.

During the Cold War, consumption in the United States wasn't only about personal gratification; it was the economic front of the great battle. When Americans went shopping, they were participating in the lifestyle that the Commies supposedly wanted to crush. When kaleidoscopic outlet malls were contrasted with Moscow's grey and barren shops, the point wasn't just that we in the West had easy access to Levi's 501s. In this narrative, our malls stood for freedom and democracy, while their empty shelves were metaphors for control and repression.

But when the Cold War ended and this ideological backdrop was yanked away, the grander meaning behind the shopping evaporated. Without ideology, shopping was just, well, shopping. The response from the corporate world was "lifestyle branding": an attempt to restore consumerism as a philosophical or political pursuit by selling powerful ideas instead of mere products. Ad campaigns began equating Benetton sweaters with fighting racism, Ikea furniture with democracy and computers with revolution.

Lifestyle branding filled shopping's "meaning" vacuum for a time, but it wasn't enough to satisfy the ambitions of the old-school Cold Warriors. Cultural exiles in a world they had created, these disgruntled hawks spent their most triumphant decade not basking in America's new uncontested power but grousing about how the U.S. had gone "soft," become feminized. It was an orgy of indulgence personified by Oprah and Bill Clinton.

But post–September 11, History is back. Shoppers are once again foot soldiers in a battle between good and evil, wearing new Stars and Stripes bras by Elita and popping special-edition red, white and blue M&M's.

When U.S. politicians urge their citizens to fight terrorism by shopping, it is about more than feeding an ailing economy. It's about once again wrapping the day-to-day in the mythic, just in time for Christmas.

America Is Not a Hamburger
America's attempt to "re-brand" itself abroad could be a worse flop than New Coke

March 2002

When the White House decided it was time to address the rising tides of anti-Americanism around the world, it didn't look to a career diplomat for help. Instead, in keeping with the Bush administration's philosophy that anything the public sector can do, the private sector can do better, it hired one of Madison Avenue's top brand managers.

As Under Secretary of State for Public Diplomacy and Public Affairs, Charlotte Beers had the assignment not to improve relations with other countries but rather to perform an overhaul of the U.S. image abroad. Beers had no previous State Department experience, but she had held the top job at both the J. Walter Thompson and Ogilvy & Mather ad agencies, and she's built brands for everything from dog food to power drills.

Now she was being asked to work her magic on the greatest branding challenge of all: to sell the United States and its "war on terrorism" to an increasingly hostile world. The appointment of an ad woman to this post understandably raised some criticism, but Secretary of State Colin L. Powell shrugged it off. "There is nothing wrong with getting somebody who knows how to sell something. We are selling a product. We need someone who can re-brand American foreign policy, re-brand diplomacy." Besides, he said, "She got me to buy Uncle Ben's rice." So why, only five months in, does the campaign for a new and improved Brand U.S.A. seem in disarray? Several of its public service announcements have been exposed for playing fast and loose with the facts. And when Beers went on a mission to Egypt in January to improve the image of the U.S. among Arab "opinion makers," it didn't go well. Muhammad Abdel Hadi, an editor at the newspaper *Al Ahram*, left his meeting with Beers frustrated that she seemed more interested in talking about vague American values than about specific U.S. policies. "No matter how hard you try to make them understand," he said, "they don't."

The misunderstanding likely stemmed from the fact that Beers views the United States' tattered international image as little more than a communications problem. Somehow, despite all the global culture pouring out of New York, Los Angeles and Atlanta, despite the fact that you can watch CNN in Cairo and *Black Hawk Down* in Mogadishu, America still hasn't managed, in Beers's words, to "get out there and tell our story."

In fact, the problem is just the opposite: America's marketing of itself has been *too* effective. Schoolchildren can recite its claims to democracy, liberty and equal opportunity as readily as they can associate McDonald's with family fun and Nike with athletic prowess. And they expect the U.S. to live up to its promises.

If they are angry, as millions clearly are, it's because they have seen the promises betrayed by U.S. policy. Despite President Bush's insistence that America's enemies resent its liberties, most critics of the U.S. don't actually object to America's stated values. Instead, they point to U.S. unilateralism in the face of international laws, widening wealth disparities, crackdowns on immigrants and human rights violations—most recently in the prison camps at Guantanamo Bay. The anger comes not only from the facts of each case but also from a clear perception of false advertising. In other words, America's problem is not with its brand—which could scarcely be stronger—but with its product.

There is another, more profound obstacle facing the relaunch of Brand U.S.A., and it has to do with the nature of branding itself. Successful branding, Allen Rosenshine, chairman and CEO of BBDO Worldwide, recently wrote in *Advertising Age*, "requires a carefully crafted message delivered with consistency and discipline." Quite true. But the values Beers is charged with selling are democracy and diversity, values that are profoundly incompatible with this "consistency and discipline." Add to this the fact that many of America's staunchest critics already feel bullied into conformity by the U.S. government (bristling at phrases like "rogue state"), and America's branding campaign could well backfire, and backfire badly.

In the corporate world, once a "brand identity" is settled on by head office, it is enforced with military precision throughout a company's operations. The brand identity may be tailored to accommodate local language and cultural preferences (like McDonald's offering hot sauce in Mexico), but its core features—aesthetic, message, logo—remain unchanged.

This consistency is what brand managers like to call "the promise" of a brand: it's a pledge that wherever you go in the world, your experience at Wal-Mart, Holiday Inn or a Disney theme park will be comfortable and familiar. Anything that threatens this homogeneity dilutes a company's overall strength. That's why the flip side of enthusiastically flogging a brand is aggressively prosecuting anyone who tries to mess with it, whether by pirating its trademarks or by spreading unwanted information about the brand on the Internet.

At its core, branding is about rigorously controlled one-way messages, sent out in their glossiest form, then hermetically sealed off from those who would turn that corporate monologue into a social dialogue. The most important tools in launching a strong brand may be research, creativity and design, but after that, libel and copyright laws are a brand's best friends.

When brand managers transfer their skills from the corporate to the political world, they invariably bring this fanaticism for homogeneity with them. For instance, when Wally Olins, co-founder of the Wolff Olins brand consultancy, was asked for his take on America's image problem, he complained that people don't have a single clear idea about what the country stands for but rather have dozens if not hundreds of ideas that "are mixed up in people's heads in a most extraordinary way. So you will often find people both admiring and abusing America, even in the same sentence."

From a branding perspective, it would certainly be tire-some if we found ourselves simultaneously admiring and abusing our laundry detergent. But when it comes to our relationship with governments, particularly the govern-ment of the most powerful and richest nation in the world, surely some complexity is in order. Having con-flicting views about the U.S.—admiring its creativity, for instance, but resenting its double standards—doesn't mean you are "mixed up," to use Olins's phrase, it means you are paying attention.

Besides, much of the anger directed at the U.S. stems from a belief—voiced as readily in Argentina as in France, in India as in Saudi Arabia—that the U.S. already demands far too much "consistency and discipline" from other nations; that beneath its stated commitment to democracy and sovereignty, it is deeply intolerant of deviations from the economic model known as "the Washington Consensus." Whether these policies, so beneficial to foreign investors, are enforced by the Washington-based International Monetary Fund or through international trade agreements, the U.S.'s critics generally feel that the world is already far too influenced by America's brand of governance (not to mention America's brands).

There is another reason to be wary of mixing the logic of branding with the practice of governance. When companies try to implement global image consistency, they look like generic franchises. But when governments do the same, they can look distinctly authoritarian. It's no coincidence that historically, the political leaders most preoccupied with branding themselves and their parties were also allergic to democracy and diversity. Think Mao Tse-tung's giant murals and Red Books, and yes, think Adolf Hitler, a man utterly obsessed with purity of image: within his party, his country, his race. This has been the ugly flip side of dictators striving for consistency of brand: centralized information, state-controlled media, re-education camps, purging of dissidents and much worse.

Democracy, thankfully, has other ideas. Unlike strong brands, which are predictable and disciplined, true democracy is messy and fractious, if not outright rebellious. Beers and her colleagues may have convinced Colin Powell to buy Uncle Ben's by creating a comforting brand image, but the United States is not made up of identical grains of rice, assembly-line hamburgers or Gap khakis.

Its strongest "brand attribute," to use a term from Beers's world, is its embrace of diversity, a value Beers is now attempting to stamp with cookie-cutter uniformity around the world, unfazed by the irony. The task is not only futile but dangerous: brand consistency and true human diversity are antithetical—one seeks sameness, the other celebrates difference; one fears all unscripted messages, the other embraces debate and dissent.

No wonder we're so "mixed up." Making his pitch for Brand U.S.A. in Beijing recently, President Bush argued that "in a free society, diversity is not disorder. Debate is not strife." The audience applauded politely. The message might have proved more persuasive if those values were better reflected in the Bush administration's communications with the outside world, both in its image and, more important, in its policies.

Because as President Bush rightly points out, diversity and debate are the lifeblood of liberty. But they are enemies of branding.

V

WINDOWS TO DEMOCRACY

In which glimmers of hope are found in a politic of
radical power decentralization, emerging from
the mountains of Chiapas and the urban squats of Italy

V

WINDOWS TO DEMOCRACY

In which glimmers of hope are found in a politic of
radical power decentralization, emerging from
the mountains of Chiapas and the urban squats of Italy

Democratizing the Movement
When activists gathered at the first World Social Forum, no single agenda could contain the diversity
March 2001

"We are here to show the world that another world is possible!" the man on stage said, and a crowd of more than ten thousand roared its approval. We were not cheering for a specific other world, just the possibility of one. We were cheering for the idea that another world could, in theory, exist.

For the past thirty years, a select group of CEOs and world leaders have met during the last week in January on a mountaintop in Switzerland to do what they presumed they were the only ones capable of doing: determining how the global economy should be governed. We were cheering because it was, in fact, the last week of January, and this wasn't the World Economic Forum in Davos, Switzerland. It was the first annual World Social Forum in Porto Alegre, Brazil. And even though we weren't CEOs or world leaders, we were still going to spend the week talking about how the global economy should be governed.

Many people said they felt history being made in that room. What I felt was something more intangible: the end of the End of History. And fittingly, Another World Is Possible was the event's official slogan. After we'd seen a year and a half of protests against the World Trade Organization, the World Bank and the International Monetary Fund, the World Social Forum was billed as an opportunity for this emerging movement to stop screaming about what it is against and start articulating what it is for.

If Seattle was, for many people, the coming-out party of a resistance movement, then, according to Soren Ambrose, policy analyst with 50 Years Is Enough, "Porto Alegre is the coming-out party for the existence of serious thinking about alternatives." The emphasis was on alternatives coming from the countries experiencing most acutely the negative effects of globalization: mass migration of people, widening wealth disparities, weakening political power.

The particular site was chosen because Brazil's Workers Party (Partido dos Trabalhadores, the PT) is in power in the city of Porto Alegre, as well as in the state of Rio Grande do Sul. The conference was organized by a network of Brazilian unions and NGOs, but the PT provided state-of-the-art conference facilities at the Catholic University of Porto Alegre and paid the bill for a star-studded roster of speakers. Having a progressive government sponsor was a departure for a group of people accustomed to being met with clouds of pepper spray, border strip searches and no-protest zones. In Porto Alegre, activists were welcomed by friendly police officers and greeters with official banners from the tourism department.

Though the conference was locally organized, it was, in part, the brainchild of ATTAC France, a coalition of unions, farmers and intellectuals that has become the most public face of the anti-globalization movement in much of Europe and Scandinavia. (ATTAC stands for Association for the Taxation of Financial Transactions for the Aid of Citizens, which, admittedly, doesn't work as well in English.) Founded in 1998 by Bernard Cassen and Susan George of the socialist monthly *Le Monde Diplomatique*, ATTAC began as a campaign for the implementation of the Tobin Tax, the proposal by the American Nobel laureate James Tobin to tax all speculative financial transactions. Reflecting its Marxist intellectual roots, the group has expressed frustration with the less coherent focus of the North American anti-corporate movement. "The failure of Seattle was the inability to come up with a common agenda, a global alliance at the world level to fight against globalization," says Christophe Aguiton of ATTAC, who helped organize the forum.

Which is where the World Social Forum came in: ATTAC saw the conference as an opportunity to bring together some of the best minds working on alternatives to neo-liberal economic policies—not just new systems of taxation but everything from sustainable farming to participatory democracy to co-operative production to independent media. From this process of information swapping ATTAC believed its "common agenda" would emerge.

The result of the gathering was something much more complicated—as much chaos as cohesion, as much division as unity. In Porto Alegre the coalition of forces that is often placed under the banner of anti-globalization began collectively to recast itself as a pro-democracy movement. In the process, the movement was also forced to confront the

weaknesses of its own internal democracy and to ask difficult questions about how decisions were being made—at the
World Social Forum itself and, more important, in the high-
stakes planning for the next round of World Trade
Organization negotiations and the proposed Free Trade Area
of the Americas.

Part of the challenge was that the organizers had no idea
how many people would be drawn to this Davos for
activists. Atila Roque, a co-ordinator of IBase, a Brazilian
policy institute and a member of the organizing committee,
explains that for months they thought they were planning
a gathering of two thousand people. Then, suddenly, there
were ten thousand, more at some events, representing a
thousand groups, from 120 countries. Most of those delegates had no idea what they were getting into: a model UN?
A giant teach-in? An activist political convention? A party?

The result was a strange hybrid of all of the above, along
with—at the opening ceremony, at least—a little bit of Vegas
floor show mixed in. On the first day of the forum, after the
speeches finished and we cheered for the end of the End of
History, the house lights went down and two giant screens
projected photographs of poverty in Rio's *favelas*. A line of
dancers appeared on stage, heads bowed in shame, feet
shuffling. Slowly, the photographs became more hopeful,
and the people on stage began to run, brandishing the tools
of their empowerment: hammers, saws, bricks, axes, books,
pens, computer keyboards, raised fists. In the final scene, a
pregnant woman planted seeds—seeds, we were told, of
another world.

What was jarring was not so much that this particular genre of utopian socialist dance had rarely been staged since the Works Progress Administration performances of the 1930s, but that it was done with such top-notch production values: perfect acoustics, professional lighting, headsets simultaneously translating the narration into four languages. All ten thousand of us were given little bags of seeds to take and plant at home. This was Socialist Realism meets *Cats*.

The forum was filled with these juxtapositions between underground ideas and Brazil's enthusiastic celebrity culture: moustachioed local politicians accompanied by glamorous wives in backless white dresses rubbing shoulders with the president of the Landless Peasants Movement of Brazil, known for chopping down fences and occupying large pieces of unused farmland. An old woman from Argentina's Mothers of the Plaza de Mayo, with her missing child's name crocheted on her white head scarf, sitting next to a Brazilian soccer star so adored that his presence provoked several hardened politicos to rip off pieces of their clothing and demand autographs. And José Bové was unable to go anywhere without a line of bodyguards protecting him from the paparazzi.

Every night the conference adjourned to an outdoor amphitheatre where musicians from around the world performed, including the Cuarteto Patria, one of the Cuban bands made famous by Wim Wenders's documentary *The Buena Vista Social Club*. Cuban anything was big here. Speakers had only to mention the existence of the island nation for the room to break out in chants of "Cuba! Cuba! Cuba!" Chanting, it must be said, was also big: not just for Cuba but for honorary president of the Workers Party Luiz Inácio "Lula" da Silva ("Lula-Lula"). José Bové earned his very own chant: "Olé, Olé, Bové, Bové," sung as a soccer stadium hymn.

One thing that wasn't so big at the World Social Forum was the United States. There were daily protests against Plan Colombia, the "wall of death" between the United States and Mexico, as well as George W. Bush's announcement that the new administration will suspend foreign aid to groups that provide information on abortion. In the workshops and lectures there was much talk of American imperialism, of the tyranny of the English language. Actual U.S. citizens, though, were notably scarce. The AFL-CIO barely had a presence (its president John Sweeney was at Davos), and there was no one there from the National Organization for Women. Even Noam Chomsky, who said the forum "offers opportunities of unparalleled importance to bring together popular forces," sent only his regrets. Public Citizen had two people in Porto Alegre, but their star, Lori Wallach, was in Davos. [*Much of this changed for the second World Social Forum in January 2002: Chomsky attended, as did Wallach, along with a larger contingent of U.S. activists.*]

"Where are the Americans?" people asked, waiting in coffee lines and around Internet link-ups. There were many theories. Some blamed the media: the U.S. press wasn't covering the event. Of fifteen hundred journalists registered, maybe ten were American, and more than half of those were from

Independent Media Centers. Some blamed Bush: the forum was held a week after his inauguration, which meant that most U.S. activists were too busy protesting the theft of the election to even think about going to Brazil. Others blamed the French: many U.S. groups didn't know about the event at all, in part because international outreach was done mainly by ATTAC, which, Christophe Aguiton acknowledged, needs "better links with the Anglo-Saxon world."

Most, however, blamed the Americans themselves. "Part of it is simply a reflection of U.S. parochialism," said Peter Marcuse, a professor of urban planning at Columbia University and a speaker at the forum. It's a familiar story: if it doesn't happen in the United States, if it isn't in English, if it's not organized by American groups, it can't be all that important—let alone be the sequel to the Battle of Seattle.

Last year, *New York Times* columnist Thomas Friedman wrote from Davos, "Every year at the World Economic Forum there is a star or theme that stands out"—the dot-coms, the Asian crisis. Last year, according to Friedman, the star of Davos was Seattle. Porto Alegre had a star as well; it was, without question, democracy: what happened to it? How do we get it back? And why isn't there more of it within the conference itself?

In workshops and on panels, globalization was defined as a mass transfer of wealth and knowledge from public to private—through the patenting of life and seeds, the privatization of water and the concentrated ownership of agricultural lands. Having this conversation in Brazil meant that these issues were not presented as shocking new inventions of a hitherto unheard-of phenomenon called "globalization"—as is often the case in the West—but as part of the continuum of colonization, centralization and loss of self-determination that began more than five centuries ago.

This latest stage of market integration has meant that power and decision making are now delegated to points even farther away from the places where the effects of those decisions are felt at the same time that ever-greater financial burdens are off-loaded to cities and towns. Real power has moved from local to state, from state to national, from national to international, until finally representative democracy means voting for politicians every few years who use that mandate to transfer national powers to the WTO and the IMF.

In response to this global crisis in representative democracy, the forum set out to sketch the possible alternatives, but before long, some rather profound questions emerged. Is this a movement trying to impose its own, more humane, brand of globalization, with taxation of global finance and more democracy and transparency in international governance? Or is it a movement against centralization and the delegation of power on principle, one as critical of left-wing, one-size-fits-all ideology as of the recipe for McGovernment churned out at forums like Davos? It's fine to cheer for the possibility of another world—but is the goal one specific other world, already imagined or is it, as the Zapatistas put it, "a world with the possibility of many worlds in it?"

On these questions there was no consensus. Some groups, those with ties to political parties, seemed to be pushing for a united international organization or party and wanted the forum to issue an official manifesto that could form a governmental blueprint. Others, those working outside traditional political channels and often using direct action, were advocating less a unified vision than a universal right to self-determination and cultural diversity.

Atila Roque was one of the people who argued forcefully that the forum should not try to issue a single set of political demands. "We are trying to break the uniformity of thought, and you can't do that by putting forward another uniform way of thinking. Honestly, I don't miss the time when we were all in the Communist Party. We can achieve a higher degree of consolidation of the agendas, but I don't think civil society should be trying to organize itself into a party."

In the end, the conference did not speak in one voice; there was no single official statement, though there were dozens of unofficial ones. Instead of sweeping blueprints for political change, there were glimpses of local democratic alternatives. The Landless Peasants Movement took delegates on day trips to reappropriated farmland used for sustainable agriculture. And then there was the living alternative of Porto Alegre itself: the city has become a showcase of participatory democracy studied around the world. In Porto Alegre, democracy isn't a polite matter of casting ballots; it's an active process, carried out in sprawling town hall meetings. The centrepiece of the Workers Party's platform is something called "the participatory budget," a system that allows direct citizen participation in the allocation of scarce city resources. Through a network of neighbourhood and issue councils, residents vote directly on which roads will be paved and which health care centres will be built. In Porto Alegre, this devolution of power has brought results that are the mirror opposite of global economic trends. For instance, rather than scaling back on public services for the poor, as is the case nearly everywhere else, the city has increased those services substantially. And rather than spiralling cynicism and voter dropout, democratic participation increases every year.

"This is a city that is developing a new model of democracy in which people don't just hand over control to the state," British author Hilary Wainwright said at the forum. "The challenge is, how do we extend that to a national and global level?"

Perhaps by transforming the anti-corporate movement into a pro-democracy movement that defends the rights of local communities to plan and manage their schools, their water and their ecology. In Porto Alegre, the most convincing responses to the international failure of representative democracy seemed to be this radical form of local participatory democracy, in cities and towns where the abstractions of global economics become day-to-day issues of homelessness, water contamination, exploding prisons and cash-starved schools. Of course, this has to take place within a context of national and international standards and resources. But what seemed to be emerging organically out of the World Social Forum (despite the best efforts of some of the organizers) was not a movement for a single global government but a vision for an increasingly connected international network of very local initiatives, each built on direct democracy.

Democracy was a topic that came up not only on the panels and in workshops but also in the hallways and in raucous late-night meetings at the youth campground. Here the subject was not how to democratize world governance or even municipal decision making—but something closer to home: the yawning "democratic deficit" of the World Social Forum itself. On one level the forum was extraordinarily open: anyone who wanted to could attend as a delegate, with no restrictions on numbers of attendees. And any group that wanted to run a workshop—alone or with another group—simply had to get a title to the organizing committee before the program was printed.

But there were sometimes sixty of these workshops going on simultaneously, while the main-stage events, where there was an opportunity to address more than a thousand delegates at a time, were dominated not by activists but by politicians and academics. Some gave rousing presentations, while others seemed painfully detached: after travelling eighteen hours or more to attend the forum, few needed to be told that "globalization is a space of dispute." It didn't help that these panels were dominated by men in their fifties, too many of them white. Nicola Bullard, deputy director of Bangkok's Focus on the Global South, half joked that the opening press conference "looked like the Last

Supper: twelve men with an average age of fifty-two." And it probably wasn't a great idea that the VIP room, an enclave of invitation-only calm and luxury, was made of glass. This in-your-face two-tiering amid all the talk of people power began to grate around the time the youth campsite ran out of toilet paper.

These grievances were symbolic of a larger problem. The organizational structure of the forum was so opaque that it was nearly impossible to figure out how decisions were made or to find ways to question those decisions. There were no open plenaries and no chance to vote on the structure of future events. In the absence of a transparent process, fierce NGO brand wars were waged behind the scenes—about whose stars would get the most airtime, who would get access to the press and who would be seen as the true leaders of this movement.

By the third day, frustrated delegates began to do what they do best: protest. There were marches and manifestos—a half-dozen at least. Beleaguered forum organizers found themselves charged with everything from reformism to racism. The Anti-Capitalist Youth contingent accused them of ignoring the important role direct action played in building the movement. Its manifesto condemned the conference as "a ruse" using the mushy language of democracy to avoid a more divisive discussion of class. The PSTU, a breakaway faction of the Workers Party, began interrupting speeches about the possibility of another world with loud chants of "Another world is not possible unless you smash capitalism and bring in socialism!" (It sounded much better in Portuguese.)

Some of this criticism was unfair. The forum accommodated an extraordinary range of views, and it was precisely this diversity that made conflicts inevitable. By bringing together groups with such different ideas about power—unions, political parties, NGOs, anarchist street protesters and agrarian reformers—the World Social Forum only made visible the tensions that are always just under the surface of these fragile coalitions.

But other questions were legitimate and have implications that reach far beyond a one-week conference. How are decisions made in this movement of movements? Who, for instance, decides which "civil society representatives" go behind the barbed wire at Davos—while protesters are held back with water cannons outside? If Porto Alegre was the anti-Davos, why were some of the most visible faces of opposition "dialoguing" in Davos?

And how do we determine whether the goal is to push for "social clauses" on labour and environmental issues in international agreements or to try to shoot down the agreements altogether? This debate—academic at previous points because there was so much resistance to social clauses from business—is now urgent. U.S. industry leaders, including Caterpillar and Boeing, are actively lobbying for the linking of trade with labour and environmental clauses, not because they want to raise standards but because these links are viewed as the key to breaking the Congressional stalemate over fast-track trade negotiating authority. By pushing for social clauses, are unions and environmentalists unwittingly helping the advancement of these negotiations, a process that will also open the door to privatization of such services as water and more aggressive protections of drug patents? Should the goal be to add on to these trade agreements or take entire sections out—water, agriculture, food safety, drug patents, education, health care? Walden Bello, executive director of Focus on the Global South, is unequivocal on this point. "The WTO is unreformable," he said at the forum, "and it is a horrible waste of money to push for reform. Labour and environmental clauses will just empower an already too-powerful organization."

There is a serious debate to be had over strategy and process, but it's difficult to see how it will unfold without bogging down a movement whose greatest strength so far has been its agility. Anarchist groups, though fanatical about process, tend to resist efforts to structure or centralize the movement. The International Forum on Globalization—the brain trust of the North American side of the movement—lacks transparency in its decision making and isn't accountable to a broad membership, even if many of its most visible members are. Meanwhile, NGOs that might otherwise collaborate often compete with one another for publicity and funding. And traditional membership-based political structures like parties and unions have been reduced to bit players in these wide webs of activism.

Perhaps the real lesson of Porto Alegre is that democracy and accountability need to be worked out first on more manageable scales—within local communities and coalitions and inside individual organizations. Without this foundation, there's not much hope for a satisfying democratic process when ten thousand activists from wildly different back-grounds are thrown on a university campus together. What has become clear is that if the one "pro" this disparate coalition can get behind is "pro-democracy," then democracy within the movement must become a high priority. The Porto Alegre Call for Mobilization clearly states that "we challenge the elite and their undemocratic processes, symbolized by the World Economic Forum in Davos." Most delegates agreed that it simply won't do to scream "Elitist!" from a glass house—or from a glass VIP lounge.

Despite the moments of open revolt, the World Social Forum ended on as euphoric a note as it began. There was cheering and chanting, the loudest coming when the orga-nizing committee announced that Porto Alegre would host the forum again next year. The plane from Porto Alegre to São Paulo on January 30 was filled with delegates dressed head-to-toe in conference-branded swag—T-shirts, baseball hats, and with mugs and bags—all bearing the utopian slo-gan Another World Is Possible. Not uncommon, perhaps, after a conference, but it did strike me as noteworthy that a couple sitting in the seats across from me were still wear-ing their WSF name tags. It was as if they wanted to hang on to that dream world, however imperfect, for as long as they could before splitting up to catch connecting flights to Newark, Paris, Mexico City, absorbed in a hub of scurrying businesspeople, duty-free Gucci bags and CNN stock news.

Rebellion in Chiapas
Subcomandante Marcos and the Zapatistas are staging a revolution that relies more on words than on bullets

March 2001

A month ago, I got an e-mail from Greg Ruggiero, the publisher of *Our Word Is Our Weapon,* a collection of writings by Subcomandante Marcos, spokesperson of the Zapatista National Liberation Army in Chiapas, Mexico. He wrote that Zapatista commanders were going on a caravan to Mexico City and that the event was "the equivalent of Martin Luther King Jr.'s March on Washington." I stared at the sentence for a long time. I have seen the clip of King's "I have a dream" speech maybe ten thousand times, though usually via advertisements selling mutual funds or cable news. Having grown up after history ended, I hadn't imagined that I might see a capital-H history moment to match it.

Next thing I knew, I was on the phone talking to airlines, cancelling engagements, making crazy excuses, mumbling about Zapatistas and Martin Luther King Jr. Who cares that it didn't make sense? All I knew was that I had to be in Mexico City on March 11, the day Marcos and the Zapatistas where scheduled to make their grand entrance.

Now would be a good time to admit that I've never been to Chiapas. I've never made the pilgrimage to the Lacandon jungle. I've never sat in the mud and the mist in La Realidad. I've never begged, pleaded or posed to get an audience with Subcomandante Marcos, the masked man, the faceless face of Mexico's Zapatista National Liberation Army. I know people who had. Lots of them. In 1994, the summer after the Zapatista rebellion, caravans to Chiapas were all the rage in North American activist circles: friends got together and raised money for second-hand vans, filled them with supplies, then drove south to San Cristobal de las Casas and left the vans behind. I didn't pay much attention at the time. Back then, Zapatista mania looked suspiciously like just another cause for guilty lefties with a Latin American fetish: another Marxist rebel army, another macho leader, another chance to go south and buy colourful textiles. Hadn't we heard this story before? Hadn't it ended badly?

But there is something different about this Zapatista caravan. First, it doesn't end in San Cristobal de las Casas; it starts there, criss-crossing the Mexican countryside before finally arriving in downtown Mexico City. The caravan, nick-named the "Zapatour" by the Mexican press, is led by the council of twenty-four Zapatista commanders, in full uniform and masks (though no weapons), including Subcomandante Marcos himself. Because it is unheard of for the Zapatista command to travel outside Chiapas (and there are vigilantes threatening deadly duels with Marcos all along the way), the Zapatour needs tight security. The Red Cross turned down the job, so protection is being provided by several hundred activists from Italy who call themselves ¡Ya Basta! (meaning "Enough is enough!"), after the defiant phrase used in the Zapatistas' declaration of war. (In the end security was provided by local groups.) Hundreds of students, small farmers and activists have joined the road show, and thousands are greeting them along the way. Unlike those early visitors to Chiapas, these travellers say they are there not because they are "in solidarity" with the Zapatistas but because they *are* Zapatistas. Some even claim to be Subcomandante Marcos himself—they say, much to the confusion of inquiring journalists, "We are all Marcos."

Perhaps only a man who never takes off his mask, who hides his real name, could lead this caravan of renegades, rebels, loners and anarchists on this two-week trek. These are people who have learned to steer clear of charismatic leaders with one-size-fits-all ideologies. These aren't party loyalists; these are members of groups that pride themselves on their autonomy and lack of hierarchy. And Marcos—with his black wool mask, intense eyes and a pipe—seems to be an anti-leader tailor-made for this suspicious, critical lot. Not only does he refuse to show his face, undercutting (and simultaneously augmenting) his own celebrity, but Marcos's story is of a man who came to his leadership not through swaggering certainty but by confronting political uncertainty, by learning to follow.

Though there is little confirmation of Marcos's real identity, the most repeated legend that surrounds him goes like this: an urban Marxist intellectual and activist, Marcos was wanted by the state and was no longer safe in the cities. He fled to the mountains of Chiapas in southeast Mexico, filled with revolutionary rhetoric and certainty, there to convert the poor indigenous masses to the cause of armed proletarian revolution against the bourgeoisie. He said the workers of the world must unite, and the Mayans just stared at him. They said they weren't workers, and besides, land wasn't property but the heart of their community. Having failed as a Marxist missionary, Marcos immersed himself in Mayan culture. The more he learned, the less he knew. Out of this process, a new kind of army emerged, the EZLN, the Zapatista National Liberation Army, which was not controlled by an elite of guerrilla commanders but by the communities themselves, through clandestine councils and open assemblies. "Our army," says Marcos, "became scandalously Indian." That meant that he wasn't a commander barking orders, but a subcomandante, a conduit for the will of the councils. His first words, in his new persona, were "Through me speaks the will of the Zapatista National Liberation Army." Further subjugating himself, Marcos says to those who seek him out that he is not a leader, but that his black mask is a mirror, reflecting each of their own struggles; that a Zapatista is anyone anywhere fighting injustice, that "We are you." Most famously, he once told a reporter that "Marcos is gay in San Francisco, black in South Africa, an Asian in Europe, a Chicano in San Ysidro, an anarchist in Spain, a Palestinian in Israel, a Mayan Indian in the streets of San Cristobal, a Jew in Germany, a Gypsy in Poland, a Mohawk in Quebec, a pacifist in Bosnia, a single woman on the Metro at 10 P.M., a peasant without land, a gang member in the slums, an unemployed worker, an unhappy student and, of course, a Zapatista in the mountains."

"This non-self," writes Juana Ponce de Leon who has edited Marcos's writings, "makes it possible for Marcos to become the spokesperson for indigenous communities. He is transparent, and he is iconographic." Yet the paradox of Marcos and the Zapatistas is that despite the masks, the non-selves, the mystery, their struggle is about the opposite of anonymity—it is about the right to be seen. When the Zapatistas took up arms and said "*¡Ya basta!*" in 1994, it was a revolt against their invisibility. Like so many others left behind by globalization, the Mayans of Chiapas had fallen off the economic map: "Below in the cities," the EZLN command stated, "we did not exist. Our lives were worth less than those of machines or animals. We were like stones, like weeds in the road. We were silenced. We were faceless." By arming and masking themselves, the Zapatistas explain, they weren't joining some *Star Trek*-like Borg universe of people without identities fighting in common cause, they were forcing the world to stop ignoring their plight, to see their long-neglected faces. The Zapatistas are "the voice that arms itself to be heard. The face that hides itself to be seen."

Meanwhile, Marcos himself—the supposed non-self, the conduit, the mirror—writes in a tone so personal and poetic, so completely and unmistakably his own, that he is constantly undercutting and subverting the anonymity that comes from his mask and pseudonym. It is often said that the Zapatistas' best weapon was the Internet, but their true secret weapon was their language. In *Our Word Is Our Weapon*, we read manifestos and war cries that are also poems, legends and riffs. A character emerges behind the mask, a personality. Marcos is a revolutionary who writes long meditative letters to Uruguayan writer Eduardo Galeano about the meaning of silence; who describes colonialism as a series of "bad jokes badly told"; who quotes Lewis Carroll, Shakespeare and Borges. Who writes that resistance takes place "anytime any man or woman rebels to the point of tearing off the clothes resignation has woven for them and cynicism has dyed grey." And who then sends whimsical mock telegrams to all of "civil society": "THE GREYS HOPE TO WIN STOP RAINBOW NEEDED URGENTLY."

Marcos seems keenly aware of himself as an irresistible romantic hero. He's an Isabel Allende character in reverse— not the poor peasant who becomes a Marxist rebel but a Marxist intellectual who becomes a poor peasant. He plays with this character, flirts with it, saying that he can't reveal his real identity for fear of disappointing his female fans. Perhaps wary that this game was getting a little out of hand, Marcos chose the eve of Valentine's Day this year to break the bad news: he is married and deeply in love, and her name is La Mar ("the Sea"—what else would it be?)

This is a movement keenly aware of the power of words and symbols. The twenty-four-strong Zapatista command had originally planned to make their grand entrance to Mexico City riding in on horseback, like indigenous conquistadors (they ended up settling on a flatbed truck filled with hay). But the caravan is more than symbolic. The goal is to address the Mexican Congress and demand that legislators pass an Indigenous Bill of Rights, a law that came out of the

Zapatistas' failed peace negotiations with former president Ernesto Zedillo. Vicente Fox, his newly elected successor who famously bragged during the campaign that he could solve the Zapatista problem "in fifteen minutes," has asked for a meeting with Marcos but has so far been refused. Not until the bill is passed, says Marcos, not until more army troops are withdrawn from Zapatista territory, not until all Zapatista political prisoners are freed. Marcos has been betrayed before and accuses Fox of staging a "simulation of peace" before the peace negotiations have even restarted.

What is clear in all this jostling for position is that something radical has changed in the balance of power in Mexico. The Zapatistas are calling the shots—which is significant, because they have lost the habit of firing shots. What started as a small, armed insurrection has in the past seven years turned into what now looks more like a peaceful mass movement. It has helped topple the corrupt seventy-one-year reign of the Institutional Revolutionary Party and has placed indigenous rights at the centre of the Mexican political agenda.

Which is why Marcos gets angry when he is looked on as just another guy with a gun: "What other guerrilla force has convened a national democratic movement, civic and peaceful, so that armed struggle becomes useless?" he asks. "What other guerrilla force asks its bases of support about what it should do before doing it? What other guerrilla force has struggled to achieve a democratic space and not taken power? What other guerrilla force has relied more on words than on bullets?"

The Zapatistas chose January 1, 1994, the day the North American Free Trade Agreement came into force, to "declare war" on the Mexican army, launching an insurrection and briefly taking control of the city of San Cristobal de las Casas and five Chiapas towns. They sent out a communiqué explaining that NAFTA, which banned subsidies to indigenous farm co-operatives, would be a "summary execution" for four million indigenous Mexicans in Chiapas, the country's poorest province.

Nearly a hundred years had passed since the Mexican revolution promised to return indigenous land through agrarian reform; after all these broken promises, NAFTA was simply the last straw. "We are the product of five hundred years of struggle . . . but today we say "¡Ya basta!" Enough is enough." The rebels called themselves Zapatistas, taking their name from Emiliano Zapata, the slain hero of the 1910 revolution who, along with a ragtag peasant army, fought for lands held by large landowners to be returned to indigenous and peasant farmers.

In the seven years since they stormed onto the scene, the Zapatistas have come to represent two forces at once: first, rebels struggling against grinding poverty and humiliation in the mountains of Chiapas and, on top of this, theorists of a new movement, another way to think about power, resistance and globalization. This theory—Zapatismo—not only turns classic guerrilla tactics inside out but much of left-wing politics on its head.

For years I have watched the Zapatistas' ideas spread through activist circles, passed along second- and third-hand:

a phrase, a way to run a meeting, a metaphor that twists your brain around. Unlike classic revolutionaries who preach through bullhorns and from pulpits, Marcos has spread the Zapatista word through riddles and long, pregnant silences. Revolutionaries who don't want power. People who must hide their faces to be seen. A world with many worlds in it.

A movement of one no and many yesses.

These phrases seem simple at first, but don't be fooled. They have a way of burrowing into the consciousness, cropping up in strange places, being repeated until they take on this quality of truth—but not absolute truth: a truth, as the Zapatistas might say, with many truths in it. In Canada, indigenous uprising is always symbolized by a blockade: a physical barrier to stop the golf course from infringing on a native burial site, to block the construction of a hydro-electric dam or to keep an old-growth forest from being logged. The Zapatista uprising was a new way to protect land and culture: rather than locking out the world, the Zapatistas flung open the doors and invited the world inside. Chiapas was transformed, despite its poverty, despite being under constant military siege, into a global gathering place for activists, intellectuals and indigenous groups.

From the first communiqué, the Zapatistas invited the international community "to watch over and regulate our battles." The summer after the uprising, they hosted a National Democratic Convention in the jungle; six thousand people attended, most from Mexico. In 1996, they hosted the first *Encuentro* for Humanity and Against Neo-Liberalism.

Some three thousand activists travelled to Chiapas to meet with others from around the world.

Marcos himself is a one-man web: he is a compulsive communicator, constantly reaching out, drawing connections between different issues and struggles. His communiqués are filled with lists of groups that he imagines are Zapatista allies: small shopkeepers, retired people and the disabled, as well as workers and campesinos. He writes to political prisoners Mumia Abu-Jamal and Leonard Peltier. He is pen pals with some of Latin America's best-known novelists. He writes letters addressed "to the people of the world."

When the uprising began, the government attempted to play down the incident as a "local" problem, an ethnic dispute easily contained. The strategic victory of the Zapatistas was to change the terms: to insist that what was going on in Chiapas could not be written off as a narrow "ethnic" struggle, that it was both specific and universal. They did this by clearly naming their enemy not only as the Mexican state but as the set of economic policies known as neo-liberalism. Marcos insisted that the poverty and desperation in Chiapas was simply a more advanced version of something happening all around the world. He pointed to the huge numbers of people who were being left behind by prosperity, whose land and work made that prosperity possible. "The new distribution of the world excludes 'minorities,'" Marcos has said. "The indigenous, youth, women, homosexuals, lesbians, people of colour, immigrants, workers, peasants; the majority who make up the world basements are presented, for power, as disposable. The distribution of the world excludes the majorities."

The Zapatistas staged an open insurrection, one that anyone could join, as long as they thought of themselves as outsiders, the shadow majority. By conservative estimates, there are now forty-five thousand Zapatista-related Web sites, based in twenty-six countries. Marcos's communiqués are available in at least fourteen languages. And then there is the Zapatista cottage industry: black T-shirts with red five-pointed stars, white T-shirts with EZLN printed in black. There are baseball hats, black EZLN ski masks, Mayan-made dolls and trucks. There are posters, including one of Comandante Ramona, the much loved EZLN matriarch, as the *Mona Lisa.*

And the Zapatista effect goes far beyond traditional solidarity support. Many who attended the first *encuentros* went on to play key roles in the protests against the World Trade Organization in Seattle and the World Bank and IMF in Washington, D.C., arriving with a new taste for direct action, for collective decision making and decentralized organizing. When the insurrection began, the Mexican military was convinced it would be able to squash the Zapatistas' jungle uprising like a bug. It sent in heavy artillery, conducted air raids, mobilized thousands of soldiers. But instead of standing on a squashed bug, the government found itself surrounded by a swarm of international activists, buzzing around Chiapas. In the study commissioned by the U.S. military from the RAND Corporation, the EZLN is studied as "a new mode of conflict—'netwar'— in which the protagonists depend on using network forms of organization, doctrine, strategy and technology."

The ring around the rebels has not protected the Zapatistas entirely. In December 1997, there was the brutal massacre at Acteal in which forty-five Zapatista supporters praying at a church were killed, most of them women and children. And the situation in Chiapas is still desperate, with thousands displaced from their homes. But it is also true that the situation would probably have been much worse, potentially with far greater intervention from the U.S. military, had it not been for international pressure. The RAND Corporation study states that the global activist attention arrived "during a period when the United States may have been tacitly interested in seeing a forceful crackdown on the rebels."

So it's worth asking what are the ideas that proved so powerful that thousands have taken it on themselves to disseminate them around the world? They have to do with power—and new ways of imagining it. For instance, a few years ago, the idea of the rebels travelling to Mexico City to address the Congress would have been impossible to contemplate. Masked guerrillas entering a hall of political power signals one thing: revolution. But Zapatistas aren't interested in overthrowing the state or naming their leader as president. If anything, they want less state power over their lives. And, besides, Marcos says that as soon as peace has been negotiated, he will take off his mask and disappear. [*When the Zapatistas finally did address the Congress, Marcos stayed outside.*]

What does it mean to be a revolutionary who is not trying

to stage a revolution? This is one of the key Zapatista paradoxes. In one of his many communiqués, Marcos writes that "it is not necessary to conquer the world. It is sufficient to make it new." He adds, "Us. Today." What sets the Zapatistas apart from your average Marxist guerrilla insurgents is that their goal is not to win control but to seize and build autonomous spaces where "democracy, liberty and justice" can thrive.

Although the Zapatistas have articulated certain key goals of their resistance (control over land, direct political representation and the right to protect their language and culture), they insist they are not interested in "the Revolution," but rather in "a revolution that makes revolution possible."

Marcos believes that what he has learned in Chiapas about non-hierarchical decision making, decentralized organizing and deep community democracy holds answers for the non-indigenous world as well—if only it were willing to listen. This is a kind of organizing that doesn't compartmentalize the community into workers, warriors, farmers and students but instead seeks to organize communities as a whole, across sectors and across generations, creating "social movements." For the Zapatistas, these autonomous zones aren't about isolationism or dropping out, sixties-style. Quite the opposite: Marcos is convinced that these free spaces, born of reclaimed land, communal agriculture, resistance to privatization, will eventually create counter-powers to the state simply by existing as alternatives.

This is the essence of Zapatismo, and explains much of its

appeal: a global call to revolution that tells you not to wait for the revolution, only to start where you stand, to fight with your own weapon. It could be a video camera, words, ideas, "hope"—all these, Marcos has written, "are also weapons." It's a revolution in miniature that says, "Yes, you can try this at home." This organizing model has spread throughout Latin America and the world. You can see it in the *centri sociali* (social centres), the anarchist squats of Italy; in the Landless Peasants' Movement of Brazil, which seizes tracts of unused farmland and uses them for sustainable agriculture, markets and schools under the slogan *Ocupar, Resistir, Producir* (Occupy, Resist, Produce). These same ideas about mobilizing the economically disappeared run through Argentina's Piquetero movement, organizations of unemployed workers whose hunger has driven them to find new ways of winning concessions from the state. In a reversal of the traditional picket line (you can't shut down factories that are already closed), the Piqueteros block roadways into the cities, often for weeks at a time, stopping traffic and the transportation of goods. Politicians are forced to come to the road pickets and negotiate, and the Piqueteros regularly win basic unemployment compensation for their members. Argentina's Piqueteros (who often can be seen sporting EZLN T-shirts) believe that in a country with 30 percent of the population out of work, unions have to start organizing whole communities, not just workers. "The new factory is the neighbourhood," says Piquetero leader Luis D'Elia. And the Zapatista ethos was forcefully expressed by the students of the National Autonomous University of Mexico during last year's long and militant occupation of their campus. Zapata once said the land belongs to those who work it; their banners blared, "WE SAY THAT THE UNIVERSITY BELONGS TO THOSE WHO STUDY IN IT."

Zapatismo, according to Marcos, is not a doctrine but "an intuition." And he is consciously trying to appeal to something that exists outside the intellect, something uncynical in us, that he found in himself in the mountains of Chiapas: wonder, a suspension of disbelief, plus myth and magic. So, instead of issuing manifestos, he tries to riff his way into this place, with long meditations, flights of fancy, dreaming out loud. This is, in a way, a kind of intellectual guerrilla warfare: Marcos won't meet his opponents on their terms, he changes the topic of conversation.

Which is why, when I arrived in Mexico for March 11, I saw something different from the big history moment I had imagined when I first got that e-mail. When the Zapatistas entered the Zócalo, the piazza in front of the legislature, with 200,000 people cheering them on, history was certainly being made, but it was a smaller, lower-case, humbler kind of history than you see in those black-and-white newsreels. A history that says, "I can't make your history for you. But I can tell you that history is yours to make."

The Zapatistas' most enthusiastic supporters that day seemed to be middle-aged women—the demographic that Americans like to call "soccer moms." They greeted the revolutionaries with chants of "You are not alone!" Some were on break from their jobs at fast-food outlets, still dressed in matching striped uniforms.

From afar, the popularity of the Zapatistas—the forty varieties of T-shirts, posters, flags and dolls—may look like mass marketing, the radical chic "branding" of an ancient culture. Yet up close, it feels like something else: genuine, anachronistic folklore. The Zapatistas have got their message out not through advertising or sound bites but through stories and symbols, painted by hand on walls, passed through word of mouth. The Internet, which mimics these organic networks, simply took this folklore and spread it around the world.

As I listened to Marcos address the crowds in Mexico City, I was struck that he didn't sound like a politician at a rally or a preacher at a pulpit, he sounded like a poet—at the world's largest poetry reading. And it occurred to me then that Marcos actually isn't Martin Luther King Jr.; he is King's very modern progeny, born of a bittersweet marriage of vision and necessity. This masked man who calls himself Marcos is the descendant of King, Che Guevara, Malcolm X, Emiliano Zapata and all the other heroes who preached from pulpits only to be shot down one by one, leaving bodies of followers wandering around blind and disoriented because they had lost their heads. And in their place, the world has a new kind of hero, one who listens more than he speaks, who preaches in riddles not in certainties, a leader who doesn't show his face, who says his mask is really a mirror. And in the Zapatistas we have not one dream of a revolution but a dreaming revolution. "This is our dream," writes Marcos, "the Zapatista paradox—one that takes away sleep. The only dream that is dreamed awake, sleepless. The history that is born and nurtured from below."

Italy's Social Centres
In reclaimed warehouses, windows of democracy are opening up

June 2001

A woman with long brown hair and a cigarette-scratched voice has a question. "What does this place look like to you?" she asks, with the help of an interpreter. "An ugly ghetto or something maybe beautiful?"

It was a trick question. We were sitting in a ramshackle squat in one of the least picturesque suburbs of Rome. The walls of the stumpy building were covered in graffiti, the ground was muddy and all around us were bulky, menacing housing projects. If any of the twenty million tourists who flocked to Rome last year had taken a wrong turn and ended up here, they would have dived for their Fodor's and fled in search of any edifice with vaulted ceilings, fountains and frescoes. But while the remains of one of the most powerful, centralized empires in history are impeccably preserved in downtown Rome, it is here, in the city's poor outskirts, that you can catch a glimpse of a new, living politics.

The squat in question is called Corto Ciccuito, one of Italy's many *centri sociali*. Social centres are abandoned buildings—warehouses, factories, military forts, schools— that have been occupied by squatters and transformed into cultural and political hubs, explicitly free from both the market and state control. By some estimates, there are 150 social centres in Italy.

The largest and oldest—Leoncavallo in Milan—is practically a self-contained city, with several restaurants, gardens, a bookstore, a cinema, an indoor skateboard ramp and a club so large it was able to host Public Enemy when the rap group came to town. These are scarce bohemian spaces in a rapidly gentrifying world, a fact that prompted the French newspaper *Le Monde* to describe them as "the Italian cultural jewel."

But the social centres are more than the best place to be on a Saturday night. They are also ground zero of a growing political militancy in Italy. In the centres, culture and politics mix easily together: a debate about direct action turns into a huge outdoor party, a rave takes place next door to a meeting about unionizing fast-food workers.

In Italy, this culture developed out of necessity. With politicians on both the left and right mired in corruption scandals, large numbers of Italian youths have understandably concluded that it is power itself that corrupts. The social centre network is a parallel political sphere that, rather than trying to gain state power, provides alternative state services—such as daycare and advocacy for refugees—at the same time as it confronts the state through direct action.

For instance, on the night I spent at Rome's Corto Ciccuito, the communal dinner of lasagne and caprese salad received a particularly enthusiastic reception because it was prepared by a chef who had just been released from jail after his arrest at an anti-fascist rally. And at Milan's Leoncavallo centre the day before, I stumbled across several members of the Tute Bianche (white overalls) poring over digital maps of Genoa in preparation for the July 2001 G8 meeting: the direct-action group, named after the uniform its members wear to protests, had just issued a "declaration of war" on the meeting in Genoa.

But such declarations aren't the most shocking things going on at the social centres. Far more surprising is the fact that these anti-authoritarian militants, defined by their rejection of party politics, have begun running for office—and winning. In Venice, Rome and Milan, prominent social centre activists, including Tute Bianche leaders, are now city councillors.

With Silvio Berlusconi's right-wing Forza Italia in office, they need to protect themselves from those who would shut down the centres. But Beppe Caccia, a Tute Bianche member and a Venetian city councillor, also says the move into municipal politics is a natural evolution of social centre theory. The nation-state is in crisis, he argues, weakened in the face of global powers and corrupt in the face of corporate ones. Meanwhile, in Italy, as in other industrialized countries, strong regional sentiments for greater decentralization have been seized by the right. In this climate, Caccia proposes a two-pronged strategy of confronting unaccountable, unrepresentative powers at the global level (for example, at the G8) while simultaneously rebuilding a more accountable and participatory politics locally (where the social centre meets the city council).

Which brings me back to the question posed in the

suburbs of Rome's mummified empire. Though it may be hard to tell at first, the social centres aren't ghettos, they are windows—not only into another way to live, disengaged from the state, but also into a new politics of engagement. And, yes, it's something maybe beautiful.

Limits of Political Parties
The leap from protest to power must be built from the ground up

December 2000

I've never joined a political party, never even been to a political convention. Last election, after being dragged by the hair to the ballot box, I was overcome by stomach pains more acute than those suffered by my friends who simply ingested their ballots. So why do I find myself agreeing that we need a new political alliance uniting Canada's progressive forces, if not a new party?

It's a debate taking place in every country where left parties are floundering but activism is on the rise, from Argentina to Italy. Canada is no exception. What's clear is that the left as it is currently constituted—a weakened and ineffective New Democratic Party [Canada's social democrats] and an endless series of street protests—is a recipe for fighting like crazy to make things not quite as bad as they would be otherwise. Which is still really bad.

The past four years have seen a wave of political organizing and militant protests. Students blockade trade meetings where politicians are bargaining their futures. In First Nations communities, from Vancouver Island to Burnt Church, New Brunswick, there is growing support for seizing back control of the forests and fisheries; people are tired of waiting for Ottawa to grant permission that the courts have already affirmed. In Toronto, the Ontario Coalition Against Poverty occupies buildings and demands the shelter that is the right of all Canadians.

There is no shortage of principled, radical organizing taking place, but turning that into a co-ordinated political force requires more than better "outreach" by the same old players. It requires wiping the slate clean, systematically identifying the constituencies that are suffering most under the current economic model—and already organizing against it most forcefully—and building a political platform from there.

I suspect such a vision wouldn't look very much like the current platform of the NDP. Listen to the most economically and socially excluded Canadians and you hear an idea entirely absent from the mainstream left: a deep distrust of the state. This distrust is based on lived experience: police harassment of dissenters and immigrants, punitive welfare offices, ineffective job training programs, patronage and corruption, and scandalous mismanagement of natural resources.

Surveying the rage directed at the federal government from across the country, the NDP has responded only with an action plan for better central management. In its policy book, there is no problem that can't be fixed with a stronger, top-down government. By consistently failing to speak to the hunger for local control, or to the well-deserved skepticism of centralized power, the NDP has yielded the entire anti-Ottawa vote to the right. It's only the hard-right Canadian

Alliance party that offers voters outside Quebec the opportunity to "send a message to Ottawa"—even if the message is simply to demand a refund on shoddy democracy in the form of a tax cut.

A national party of the left could articulate a different vision, one founded on local democracy and sustainable economic development. But before that can happen, the left needs to come to grips with how Canadians see government. It needs to listen to the voices on native reserves and in non-native resource communities where the common ground is a rage at government—federal and provincial—for culpably mismanaging the land and the oceans from urban offices. Government programs designed to "develop" the regions are utterly discredited across the country. Federal initiatives to get fishermen into ecotourism, for instance, or farmers into information technologies are regarded as make-work projects, unresponsive and, at times, destructive to the real needs of communities.

Frustration with botched central planning is not just an issue in rural Canada and, of course, Quebec. Urban centres across the country are being bundled into megacities against their will, just as hospitals where cutting-edge programs once thrived are being amalgamated into inefficient medical factories. And if you listen to the teachers having standardized testing rammed down their throats by half-literate politicians, you hear the same resentment at faraway power, the same calls for local control and deeper, day-to-day democracy.

All these local battles are, at their root, about people

watching power shift to points farther and farther away from where they live and work: to the WTO, to unaccountable multinationals, but also to more centralized national, provincial and even municipal governments. These people are not asking for more enlightened central planning, they are asking for the tools, both financial and democratic, to control their destinies, to use their expertise, to build diverse economies that are genuinely sustainable. And they have plenty of ideas.

On the west coast of Vancouver Island, they are calling for community fish-licence banks, bodies that would keep fishing rights in the community rather than selling them back to Ottawa or to corporate fleets. Native and non-native fishermen, meanwhile, are doing end runs around the Department of Fisheries and Oceans to try to save the salmon fishery by rehabilitating spawning grounds and protecting hatcheries. In other parts of British Columbia, they talk of community forest licences: taking away Crown land from multinational forestry companies that are only interested in volume-based logging and placing sustainable forest management in the hands of local communities.

Even in Newfoundland, long written off by Ottawa as Canada's welfare case, there was talk during the 2000 election of renegotiating federalism to regain control over the province's rich energy reserves and what's left of the fishery. It's the same message from Inuit leaders determined to ensure that as the oil and gas prospectors move into their territories once again, the benefits go toward regional development rather than simply enriching multinational corporations.

In many ways, these spontaneous, grassroots ideas and experiments are the antithesis of the free-trade model pushed by the federal Liberals, which insists that increased foreign investment is the key to all our prosperity, even if it means trading away democratic powers in the process. These communities want the opposite: beefed-up local control so they can do more with less.

This vision also presents a clear alternative to the anti-immigrant and regional resentments being peddled by right-wing populists. Sure, tax cuts and scapegoats aren't bad consolation prizes if nothing else is on offer. But there is clearly a deep desire in this country to continue to act collectively, to pool resources and knowledge and build something better than what we can achieve as individuals.

This presents a tremendous opportunity for the left, an opportunity that has been entirely wasted by the NDP and by social democratic parties across Europe. There is a wide-open space in the political landscape for a new political coalition that looks at the calls for localization and doesn't see a dire threat to national unity but the building blocks for a unified—and diverse—culture. In these calls for self-determination, grassroots democracy and ecological sustainability are the pieces of a new political vision that includes many Canadians who have never before been represented by the so-called left.

Right now, we have federal parties that try to hold this country together against its will, and regional parties that pit the country against itself at its peril. What's needed is a political force capable of showing us not the differences but the connections among these struggles for localization.

That would mean chucking out some of the traditional left's most basic ideas about how to organize a country. After all, the thread that connects municipal rights to sustainable resource management, as well as Quebec sovereignty to native self-government, is not a stronger central state. It is the desire for self-determination, economic sustainability and participatory democracy.

Decentralizing power doesn't mean abandoning strong national and international standards—and stable, equitable funding—for health care, education, affordable housing and environmental protections. But it does mean that the mantra of the left needs to change from "increase funding" to "empower the grassroots"—in towns, on native reserves, at schools, in resource communities, in workplaces.

Bringing these, and other, forces together would draw out simmering conflicts between natives and non-natives, unions and environmentalists, urban and rural communities—as well as between the white face of the Canadian left and the darker face of Canadian poverty. To overcome these divisions, what is needed is not a new political party—at least not yet—but a new political process, one with enough faith in democracy to let a political mandate emerge.

Creating this process would be an arduous long-term project. But it would be worthwhile. Because it is in the connections between these long-ignored issues and off-the-map communities that outlines of a powerful, and genuinely new, political alternative can be found.

From Symbols to Substance
After September 11, concrete alternatives to both religious and economic fundamentalism are needed more than ever

October 2001

In Toronto, the city where I live, housing-rights activists defied the logic that anti-corporate protests died on September 11. They did it by "shutting down" the business district last week. This was no polite rally: the posters advertising the event had a picture of skyscrapers outlined in red—the perimeters of the designated direct-action zone. It was almost as if September 11 had never happened. Sure, the organizers knew that targeting office buildings and stock exchanges isn't very popular right now, especially just an hour's plane journey from New York. But then again, the Ontario Coalition Against Poverty wasn't very popular before September 11. The political group's last action involved "symbolically evicting" the provincial minister of Housing from his office (his furniture was moved into the street), so you can imagine how much support it has from the press.

In other ways, too, September 11 changed little for OCAP: the nights are still getting colder and a recession is still looming. It didn't change the fact that many will die on the streets this winter, as they did last winter, and the one before that, unless more beds are found immediately.

But for other groups, those perhaps more interested in public opinion, September 11 changes a great deal. In North America at least, campaigns that rely on targeting—even peacefully—powerful symbols of capitalism find themselves in an utterly transformed semiotic landscape. After all, the attacks were acts of real and horrifying terror, but they were also acts of symbolic warfare, instantly understood as such. As many commentators put it, the towers were not just any buildings, they were "symbols of American capitalism."

Of course, there is little evidence that America's most wanted Saudi-born millionaire has a grudge against capitalism (if Osama bin Laden's rather impressive global export network stretching from cash-crop agriculture to oil pipelines is any indication, it seems unlikely). And yet for the movement that some people describe as being "anti-globalization," and others call "anti-capitalist" (and I tend to just sloppily call "the movement"), it's difficult to avoid discussions about symbolism: about all the anti-corporate signs and signifiers—the culture-jammed logos, the guerrilla-warfare stylings, the choices of brand-name and political targets—that make up the movement's dominant metaphors. Many political opponents of anti-corporate activism are using the symbolism of the World Trade Center and Pentagon attacks to argue that young activists, playing at guerrilla war, have now been caught out by a real war. The obituaries are already appearing in newspapers around the world: "Anti-Globalization Is So Yesterday" reads a typical headline. The movement is, according to *The Boston Globe*, "in tatters." Is that true?

Our activism has been declared dead before. Indeed, it is declared dead with ritualistic regularity before and after every mass demonstration: our strategies apparently discredited, our coalitions divided, our arguments misguided. And yet those demonstrations have kept growing larger, from 50,000 in Seattle to 300,000, by some estimates, in Genoa.

At the same time, it would be foolish to pretend nothing has changed since September 11. This struck me recently, looking at a slide show I had been pulling together before the attacks. It is about how anti-corporate imagery is increasingly being absorbed by corporate marketing. One slide shows a group of activists spray-painting the window of a Gap outlet during the anti-WTO protests in Seattle. The next shows Gap's recent window displays featuring its own prefab graffiti—the word "Independence" sprayed in black. And the next is a frame from Sony PlayStation's State of Emergency game featuring cool-looking anarchists throwing rocks at evil riot cops protecting the fictitious American Trade Organization. Now all I can see is how these snapshots from the image wars have been instantly overshadowed, blown away by September 11 like so many toy cars and action figures on a disaster-movie set.

Despite the altered landscape—or because of it—it bears remembering why this movement chose to wage symbolic struggles in the first place. OCAP's decision to "shut down" the business district came from a set of very specific circumstances. Like so many others trying to get issues of economic inequality on the political agenda, the people the group represents felt that they had been discarded, left outside the paradigm, disappeared and reconstituted as a panhandling or squeegee problem requiring tough new legislation. They realized that what they had to confront was not just a local political enemy or even a particular trade law but an economic paradigm—the broken promise of deregulated, trickle-down capitalism.

Thus the modern activist challenge: how do you organize against an ideology so vast that it has no edges; so everywhere that it seems nowhere? Where is the site of resistance for those with no workplaces to shut down, whose communities are constantly being uprooted? What do we hold on to when so much that is powerful is virtual—currency trades, stock prices, intellectual property and arcane trade agreements?

The short answer, at least before September 11, was that you grab anything you can get your hands on: the brand image of a famous multinational, a stock exchange, a meeting of world leaders, a single trade agreement or, in the case of the Toronto group, the banks and corporate headquarters that are the engines that power this agenda. Anything that, even fleetingly, makes the intangible actual, the vastness somehow human-scale. In short, you find symbols and you hope they become metaphors for change.

For instance, when the United States launched a trade war against France for daring to ban hormone-laced beef, José Bové and the French Farmers' Confederation didn't get the world's attention by screaming about import duties on Roquefort cheese. They did it by "strategically dismantling" a McDonald's.

Many activists have learned over the past decade that the blind spot many Westerners have concerning international affairs can be overcome by linking campaigns to famous brands—an effective, if often problematic, weapon against parochialism. These corporate campaigns have, in turn, opened back doors into the arcane world of international trade and finance, to the World Trade Organization, the World Bank and, for some, to a questioning of capitalism itself.

These tactics have also proven to be an easy target in turn. After September 11, politicians and pundits around the world instantly began spinning the terrorist attacks as part of a continuum of anti-American and anti-corporate violence: first the Starbucks window, then, presumably, the World Trade Center. *New Republic* editor Peter Beinart seized on a single post to an anti-corporate Internet chat room that asked if the attacks were committed by "one of us." Beinart concluded that "the anti-globalization movement . . . is, in part, a movement motivated by hatred of the United States"—immoral with the U.S. under attack. Reginald Dale, writing in *The International Herald Tribune*, went furthest in the protester as terrorist equation. "While they are not deliberately setting out to slaughter thousands of innocent people, the protesters who want to prevent the holding of meetings like those of the IMF or the WTO are seeking to advance their political agenda through intimidation, which is a classic goal of terrorism."

In a sane world, rather than fuelling such a backlash, the terrorist attacks would raise questions about why U.S.

intelligence agencies were spending so much time spying on Reclaim the Streets and Independent Media Centres instead of on the terrorist networks plotting mass murder. Unfortunately, it seems clear that the crackdown on activism that predated September 11 will only intensify, with heightened surveillance, infiltration and police violence. The attacks could well, I fear, also cost this movement some of its political victories. Funds committed to the AIDS crisis in Africa are disappearing, and commitments to expand debt cancellation will likely follow. Now aid is being used as payola for countries that sign up for America's war.

And free trade, long facing a public relations crisis, is fast being rebranded, like shopping and baseball, as a patriotic duty. According to U.S. Trade Representative Robert Zoellick, the world needs a new campaign to "fight terror with trade." In an essay in *The New York Times Magazine,* business author Michael Lewis makes a similar conflation between freedom fighting and free trading when he explains that the traders who died were targeted as "not merely symbols but also practitioners of liberty. . . . They work hard, if unintentionally, to free others from constraints. This makes them, almost by default, the spiritual antithesis of the religious fundamentalist, whose business depends on a denial of personal liberty in the name of some putatively higher power."

The battle lines have been drawn: trade equals freedom, anti-trade equals fascism.

As a movement, our civil liberties, our advances, our usual strategies—all are now in question. But this crisis also opens up new possibilities. As many have pointed out, the challenge for social justice movements is to demonstrate that justice and equality are the most sustainable strategies against violence and fundamentalism. What does that mean in practice? Well, Americans are finding out fast what it means to have a public health care system so overburdened that it cannot handle the flu season, let alone an anthrax outbreak. Despite a decade of pledges to safeguard the U.S. water supply from bioterrorist attack, almost nothing has been done by its overburdened Environmental Protection Agency. The food supply is even more vulnerable, with inspectors managing to check about 1 percent of food imports—hardly a safeguard against rising fears of "agroterrorism."

In this "new kind of war," terrorists are finding their weapons in our tattered public infrastructures. This is true not only in rich countries such as the U.S. but also in poor countries, where fundamentalism has been spreading rapidly. Where debt and war have ravaged infrastructure, fanatical sugar daddies like bin Laden are able to swoop in and start providing basic services that should be the job of government: roads, schools, health clinics, even basic sanitation. In Sudan, it was bin Laden who built the road that enabled the construction of the Talisman oil pipeline, pumping resources to the government for its brutal ethnic war. The extreme Islamic seminaries in Pakistan that indoctrinated so many Taliban leaders thrive precisely because they fill a huge social welfare gap. In a country that spends 90 percent of its budget on its military and debt—and a pittance on education—the *madrassas* offer not only free classrooms but also food and shelter for poor children.

In understanding the spread of terrorism—north and south—questions of infrastructure and public funding are unavoidable. And yet what is the response from politicians so far? More of the same: tax breaks for businesses and further privatized services. On the same day that *The International Herald Tribune* ran the front-page headline "New Terrorism Front Line: The Mailroom," it was announced that European Union governments had agreed to open their postal delivery markets to private competition.

The debate about what kind of globalization we want is not "so yesterday"; it has never been more urgent. Many campaign groups are now framing their arguments in terms of "common security"—a welcome antidote to the narrow security mentality of fortress borders and B-52s that are so far doing such a spectacularly poor job of protecting anyone. Yet we cannot be naive, as if the very real threat of more slaughtering of innocents will disappear through political reform alone. There needs to be social justice, but there also needs to be justice for the victims of these attacks and practical prevention of future ones. Terrorism is indeed an international threat, and it did not begin with the attacks in the U.S. Many who support the bombing of Afghanistan do so grudgingly: for some, the bombs seem to be the only weapons available, however brutal and imprecise. But this paucity of options is partly a result of U.S. resistance to a range of more precise and potentially effective international instruments.

Like a standing international criminal court, which the U.S. opposes, fearing that its own war heroes might face prosecution. Like the Comprehensive Test Ban Treaty on nuclear weapons, also a no-go. And all the other treaties the U.S. has refused to ratify, on land mines, small arms and so much else that would have helped us cope with a heavily militarized state such as Afghanistan. As Bush invites the world to join America's war, sidelining the UN and the international courts, we in this movement need to become passionate defenders of true multilateralism, rejecting once and for all the label "anti-globalization." Bush's "coalition" does not represent a genuinely global response to terrorism but the internationalization of one country's foreign policy objectives—the trademark of U.S. international relations, from the WTO negotiating table to Kyoto. We can make these connections not as anti-Americans but as true internationalists.

Is the outpouring of mutual aid and support that the tragedies of September 11 have elicited so different from the humanitarian goals to which this movement aspires? The street slogans—People before Profit, The World Is Not for Sale—have become self-evident and viscerally felt truths for many in the wake of the attacks. There are questions about why the bailouts for airlines aren't going to the workers losing their jobs. There is growing concern about the volatilities of deregulated trade. There is a groundswell of appreciation for public sector workers of all kinds. In short, "the commons"—the public sphere, the public good, the noncorporate—is undergoing something of a rediscovery in the U.S., of all places.

Those concerned with changing minds (and not simply

winning arguments) should seize this moment to connect these humane reactions to the many other arenas in which human needs must take precedence over corporate profits, from AIDS treatment to homelessness.

This would require a dramatic change in activist strategy, one based much more on substance than on symbols. Fortunately, it is already happening. For more than a year, the largely symbolic activism outside summits and against individual corporations has faced challenges within movement circles. There is much that is unsatisfying about fighting a war of symbols: the glass shatters in the McDonald's window, the meetings are driven to ever more remote locations—but so what? It's still only symbols, facades, representations.

Before September 11, a new mood of impatience was already taking hold, an insistence on putting forward social and economic alternatives that address the roots of injustice, from land reform to slavery reparations to participatory democracy.

After September 11, the task is even more clear: the challenge is to shift a discourse around the vague notion of globalization into a specific debate about democracy. In a period of "unprecedented prosperity," countries around the world were told they had no choice but to slash public spending, revoke labour laws, rescind environmental protections—deemed illegal trade barriers—and defund schools. All this was apparently necessary to make them trade ready, investment friendly, world competitive.

The task now is to measure the euphoric promises of globalization—that it would bring general prosperity, greater development and more democracy—against the reality of these policies. We need to prove that globalization—this version of globalization—has been built on the back of local human and ecological welfare.

Too often, these connections between global and local are not made. Instead, we sometimes seem to have two activist solitudes. On the one hand, there are the international globalization activists who seem to be fighting faraway issues, unconnected to people's day-to-day struggles. Because they don't represent the local realities of globalization, they are too easily dismissed as misguided university students or professional activists. On the other hand, there are thousands of community-based organizations fighting daily struggles for survival, or for the preservation of the most elementary public services. Their campaigns are often dismissed as purely local, even insignificant, which is why most grassroots activists understandably feel burnt out and demoralized.

The only clear way forward is for these two forces to merge. What is now the anti-globalization movement must turn into thousands of local movements, fighting the way neo-liberal politics are playing out on the ground: homelessness, wage stagnation, rent escalation, police violence, prison explosion, criminalization of immigrants and refugees, the erosion of public schools and imperilling of the water supply. At the same time, the local movements fighting privatization and deregulation on the ground need to link their campaigns into a large global movement, one capable of showing where their particular issues fit into an international economic agenda being enforced around the world. What is needed is a political framework that can both take on corporate power and control internationally, and empower local organizing and self-determination.

Key to this process is developing a political discourse that is not afraid of diversity, that does not try to cram every political movement into a single model. Neo-liberal economics is biased at every level toward centralization, consolidation, homogenization. It is a war waged on diversity. Against it, we need a movement that encourages and fiercely protects the right to diversity: cultural diversity, ecological diversity, agricultural diversity—and yes, political diversity as well: different ways of doing politics. The goal is not better faraway rules and rulers but close-up democracy on the ground.

To get to this place, we need to make room for the voices—coming from Chiapas, Porto Alegre, Kerala—showing that it is possible to challenge imperialism while embracing plurality, progress and deep democracy. In 1998, Benjamin Barber described a pending global battle in his book *Jihad vs. McWorld*. Our task, never more pressing, is to point out that there are more than two worlds available, to expose all the invisible worlds between the economic fundamentalism of "McWorld" and the religious fundamentalism of "Jihad."

The strength of this movement of movements has been that it offers a real alternative to the homogenization and centralization represented by globalization. No one sector or country can claim it, no one intellectual elite can control it, and that is its secret weapon. A truly diverse global movement, one that is rooted everywhere that abstract economic theory becomes a local reality, doesn't have to be outside of every summit, slamming head-on into vastly more powerful institutions of military and economic might. Instead, it can surround them from all directions. Because, as we have seen, the police can wage war on a protest, they can learn to contain it, they can build higher fences. But there is no fence big enough to contain a true social movement, because it is everywhere.

Maybe the image wars are coming to a close. A year ago, I visited the University of Oregon to do a story on anti-sweatshop activism at the campus that is nicknamed Nike U. There I met student activist Sarah Jacobson. Nike, she told me, was not the target of her activism but a tool, a way to access a vast and often amorphous economic system. "It's a gateway drug," she said cheerfully.

For years, we in this movement of movements have fed off our opponents' symbols—their brands, their office towers, their photo-opportunity summits. We have used them as rallying cries, as focal points, as popular education tools. But these symbols were never the real targets; they were the levers, the handles. The symbols were only ever windows. It's time to move through them.

Acknowledgments

When I first decided to collect these articles and essays into a book, my hope was that the project could raise funds for activist organizations whose brave front-line work makes my writing possible. My agents, Bruce Westwood and Nicole Winstanley, took this vague hope and negotiated it into a reality, with the expert and ongoing help of Brian Iler, Alisa Palmer and Clayton Ruby. I am tremendously grateful to my English-language publishers who have all made the remarkable commitment of donating a portion of this book's proceeds to the Fences and Windows Fund, which will raise money for activist legal defence and popular education about global democracy. Louise Dennys, Susan Roxborough, Philip Gwyn Jones and Frances Coady embraced this unconventional idea from the start.

My greatest editorial debt goes to Debra Levy. In addition to helping me research many of these columns, Debra took charge of editing this collection with unswerving commitment and sensitivity, always keeping her eye on both the big picture and on the smallest details. Louise Dennys courageously resisted the temptation to demand a complete rewrite and instead, with the lightest of hands, managed to change everything. The manuscript was further improved, polished, and double-checked by Damián Tarnopolsky, Deirdre Molina and Alison Reid, and designed by Scott Richardson.

My husband, Avi Lewis, edited each piece when I first wrote them, no matter how many miles or time zones separated us. Kyle Yamada was the personal and editorial backup for Debra Levy and we are both most grateful. My parents, Bonnie and Michael Klein, also read drafts and offered comments. As the datelines on these articles attest, I have spent most of the past two and half years everywhere but home. This wandering has only been possible because my colleague Christina Magill has been holding down the fort, facing down every logistical challenge with baffling serenity and ingenuity.

I worked with many exceptional newspaper and magazine editors on the articles in this book: Patrick Martin, Val Ross and Larry Orenstein at *The Globe and Mail;* Seumas Milne and Katharine Viner at *The Guardian;* Betsy Reed and Katrina van den Heuvel at *The Nation;* Jesse Hirsh and Andréa Schmidt at www.nologo.org; Joel Bleifuss at *In These Times;* Michael Albert at Znet; Tania Molina at *La Jornada;* Håkan Jaensson at *Aftonbladet;* Giovanni De Mauro at *Internazionale;* and Sander Pleij at *De Groene Amsterdammer.*

It was Richard Addis and Bruce Westwood who thought it would be a good idea for me to write a weekly newspaper column during the most hectic years of my life. As I scrambled to meet each deadline, e-mailing from airport pay phones, tear-gas-filled community centres and crummy hotels with rotary lines, I must confess that I questioned their judgment more than once. Now I see what they have given me: a weekly record of a remarkable chapter in our history.

Credits

I Windows of Dissent

"Seattle" was originally published in *The New York Times* on December 2, 1999.

"Washington, D.C.: Capitalism comes out of the closet. Before" was originally published in *The Globe and Mail* on April 12, 2000.

"Washington, D.C.: Capitalism comes out of the closet. After" was originally published in *The Globe and Mail* on April 19, 2000.

"What's Next?" was originally published in *The Nation* on July 10, 2000.

"Prague: The alternative to capitalism isn't communism, it's decentralized power" was originally published in *The Globe and Mail* on September 27, 2000.

"Toronto: Anti-poverty activism and the violence debate" was originally published in *The Globe and Mail* on June 21, 2000.

II Fencing in Democracy:
   Trade and Trade-Offs

"The Free Trade Area of the Americas" was originally published in *The Globe and Mail* on March 28, 2001.

"IMF Go to Hell" was originally published in *The Globe and Mail* on March 16, 2002.

"No Place for Local Democracy" was originally published in *The Globe and Mail* on February 28, 2001.

"The War on Unions" was originally published in *The Globe and Mail* on January 17, 2001.

"The NAFTA Track Record" was originally published in *The Globe and Mail* on April 18, 2001.

"Post–September 11 Postscript" was originally published in *The Globe and Mail* on December 12, 2001.

"Higher Fences at the Border" was originally published in *The Globe and Mail* on November 22, 2000.

The Market Swallows the Commons

"Genetically Altered Rice" was originally published in *The Globe and Mail* on August 2, 2000.

"Genetic Pollution" was originally published in *The Globe and Mail* on June 20, 2001.

"Foot-and-Mouth's Sacrificial Lambs" was originally published in *The Globe and Mail* on March 7, 2001.

"The Internet as Tupperware Party" was originally published in *The Globe and Mail* on November 8, 2000.

"Co-opting Dissent" was originally published in *The Globe and Mail* on May 31, 2001.

"Economic Apartheid in South Africa" was originally published in *The Globe and Mail* on November 21, 2001.

"Poison Policies in Ontario" was originally published in *The Globe and Mail* on June 14, 2000.

"America's Weakest Front" was originally published in *The Globe and Mail* on October 26, 2001.

III Fencing in the Movement: Criminalizing Dissent

"Cross-Border Policing" was originally published in *The Globe and Mail* on May 31, 2000.

"Pre-emptive Arrest" was originally published in *The Globe and Mail* on June 7, 2000.

"Surveillance" was originally published in *The Globe and Mail* on August 30, 2000.

"Fear Mongering" was originally published in *The Globe and Mail* on March 21, 2001.

"Infiltration" was originally published in *The Globe and Mail* on April 21, 2001.

"Indiscriminate Tear-Gassing" was originally published in *The Globe and Mail* on April 25, 2001.

"Manufacturing Threats" was originally published in *The Globe and Mail* on September 5, 2001.

"Stuck in the Spectacle" was originally published in *The Globe and Mail* on May 2, 2001.

IV Capitalizing on Terror

"New Opportunists" was originally published in *The Globe and Mail* on October 3, 2001.

"Kamikaze Capitalists" was originally published in *The Globe and Mail* on November 7, 2001.

"The Terrifying Return of Great Men" was originally published in *The Globe and Mail* on December 19, 2001.

"America Is Not a Hamburger" was originally published in *The Los Angeles Times* on March 10, 2002.

V Windows to Democracy

"Democratizing the Movement" was originally published in *The Nation* on March 19, 2001.

"Rebellion in Chiapas" was originally published in *The Guardian* on March 3, 2001.

"Italy's Social Centres" was originally published in *The Globe and Mail* on June 7, 2001.

"Limits of Political Parties" was originally published in *The Globe and Mail* on December 20, 2000.

"From Symbols to Substance" was originally published in *The Nation* on October 22, 2001.

Index

Born in Montreal in 1970, Naomi Klein is an award-winning journalist and the author of the international bestseller, *No Logo: Taking Aim at the Brand Bullies*. Translated into twenty-five languages, *No Logo* was dubbed a "movement bible" by *The New York Times*. In 2001, *No Logo* won the Canadian National Business Book Award and Le Prix Méditations in France.

Naomi Klein's articles have appeared in numerous publications, including *The Nation, The New Statesman, The New York Times* and *Ms. Magazine*. She writes an internationally syndicated column for *The Globe and Mail* in Canada and *The Guardian* in Britain.

For the past six years, Ms. Klein has traveled throughout North America, Asia, Latin America, and Europe, tracking the rise of anticorporate activism. She is a frequent media commentator and university guest lecturer. In the fall of 2002, Ms. Klein was a Miliband Fellow at the London School of Economics.